Fire Women

This book is a must-read. It's biblically based, informative, and practical. No one can speak to a woman like another woman, and Joanna is not afraid to tackle the hard subjects, bringing insight and wisdom into issues that matter. She speaks from experience and from a life sold out to Jesus Christ. I'm going to make sure that all my granddaughters read this book!

—Rev. Greg Speck, author of *Sex: It's Worth Waiting For, Living for Jesus beyond the Spiritual High, Built to Last,* and *Mustard Seeds on Youth Ministry*

I've seen firsthand the unnecessary pain and trauma experienced in today's culture concerning dating relationships during my twenty-four years of working in crisis pregnancy centers across the country. Joanna's insightful book shares the crucial key of how women can live their lives without apology—and without regret.

—Maggie Downing, executive director of various pregnancy centers across the United States

Although *Fire Women* is a book written specifically for women, its powerful underlying message is universal. We have become a culture that values self-gratification above all else. Unfortunately, this self-centeredness severely damages individuals, destroys relationships, and ultimately undermines society overall. Joanna Sanders compellingly shares her story of how God changed not only her desires, but her heart and entire life, discovering the principle that surrendering our lives to Jesus gives us a far more fulfilling life than we could ever hope to find through self-seeking strategies. This superb book reminds us that God's ways and wisdom are always best.

—Dan Brownell, editor,
Today's Christian Living and *Today's Pastor*

Balancing biblical accuracy, practical discipleship, and candid personal experience, Joanna Sanders gives a comprehensive package full of powerful truth. *Fire Women* is a must-read for any single woman wanting to honor God and walk in victory.

—Nancy Kaser, author of
CROWN: 30 Wife-Changing Lessons

FIRE WOMEN

*Sexual Purity & Submission
for the Passionate Woman*

2ND EDITION

FIRE WOMEN

2ND EDITION

JOANNA SANDERS

Foreword by Dr. Joey Cook

ISBN 13: 978-1-7342932-7-2 (Paperback)

To the God who sees me

You were shown these things so that you might
know that the Lord is God; besides Him there is no
other. From heaven He made you hear His voice to
discipline you. On earth He showed you His great
fire, and you heard His words from out of the fire.
(Deut. 4:35–36)

Contents

Foreword

I believe the single greatest need for young Christians today is to formulate a biblical worldview in an ever-changing culture that often rejects any sort of absolute truth. Joanna Sanders's book, *Fire Women*, accomplishes this very purpose.

Her book has appeared on the scene at a much-needed time at the intersection of an evolving culture and the church. We are living in a day where these shifts regarding sexuality must be addressed. The church can no longer be silent on issues of sexuality. As the pastor of a local church and the leader of a regional network of churches that exists statewide, I take personal responsibility for our silence. Not only does this book address the nuances of sexuality that have often failed to be mentioned in the church, but it does so in a way that will appeal to those who are seeking to articulate biblical perspectives on these polarizing issues.

There seems to be a lot of noise circulating in modern thought regarding sexuality and theology. Many millennials have become "Instagram famous" through their bold posts celebrating their openly gay lifestyles while touting their faith in Christ. The purpose of this foreword is not to debate those stands but rather to shine a light on God's truth—the currently less celebrated approach to sexuality. Joanna's solid biblical basis, which she received through her education and ongoing con- secration, shines through in *Fire Women*. This attribute is very appealing in this particular genre of literature. Although I'm sure there is other content available with sound doctrine as the basis, I am certain that Joanna's openness and vulnerability on the subject will bring a unique perspective to this conversation. I have always admired that about her writing and coaching. Joanna writes from a perspective that is grounded in the gospel, and she does so with wisdom, grace, and eloquence.

In *Fire Women*, we hear from an author who is fulfilling the most difficult yet critical command of our Lord, one that requires a "death to self." When we walk with the Spirit, we are never alone, and the Holy Spirit will do that which we are unable.

This book reminds us of Titus 2:3–5:

Likewise, teach the older women to be reverent in the way they live, not to be slanderers or addicted to much wine, but to teach what is good. Then they can urge the younger women to love their husbands and children, to be self-controlled and pure, to be busy at home, to be kind, and to be subject to their husbands, so that no one will malign the word of God.

Joanna Sanders is a wise woman who has struggled with understanding her own passion and may continue to struggle from time to time. However, she is a real-life study of a "fire woman" who desires that younger women follow the older women in yielding the desires of their flesh, placing Jesus as the King of their hearts, walking together as sisters in Christ, and all the while pointing each other back to our King.

Thank you, Joanna, for your bravery, your friendship, and your voice at a much-needed time in history.
—Dr. Pastor Joey and Syndal Cook,
City Church, Conway, Arkansas

Introduction

When I was in college, I took up training in the martial arts. I admit as I progressed through the ranks, it felt empowering to see my skills surpass those of even some of the men around me. I became the president of the karate club and was diligent in my training toward a black belt. My sensei was one of the first people used boldly in my life to teach me the importance of humility. In one unforgettable lesson, my sensei said, "The closer you get to black belt, the more you realize all that you don't know."

Almost twenty years later I have grown to understand the deep value in this lesson. It wasn't until I got close enough to my Master (the Lord Jesus Christ) that I started to appreciate the reflection of all that I am not. My true lesson in this started when I got saved in 2012, and I have been deep in this training since then.

So at this point I can tell you that I feel unqualified to write this book. It isn't the only one to discuss sexual purity or to share a story of moving out of the darkness into the light, and it's certainly not the only book about submission. In fact, I'm sure many authors have handled these topics better than I have. (I have tried to highlight some of them within this text.) And without doubt, there's not a book available that can speak truth more powerfully than the Word of God, the Holy Bible. I believe the Bible to be inerrant and infallible. My book certainly is not.

Fire Women is, however, a testimony ultimately to my faith in Jesus Christ as Lord and the hope that He will use this, and my unique voice, to inspire others through His work in my life. I pray that my readers may come alongside me, allowing me to share how I learned how to turn my world-focused passion into God-focused passion—even through deep struggles.

Amazingly enough, this journey of redemption begins on April 1, 2012, and comes to conclusion on April 1, 2017. This is a story of five years of seeking God, stumbling, submitting, and finding what it truly means to live a passionate life. This is the raw testimony of what led me to seek and find God's rules for dealing with sexual desire, the boundaries of affection before marriage, and what it means for a woman like me to submit. Before I became a Christian, I was a very different woman.

From my early preteen years, I was surrounded with the "innocent" sexual images from boy magazines like *Teen Beat* and *Tiger Beat*, which were all the rage in the '80s. While they featured centerfolds and pinups of the latest teen crush, they were also coupled with articles describing what these guys desired on a first date and mail-in contests offering a lucky winner the chance to win a date with Chad or Kirk. (A shout-out to Kirk Cameron. I appreciate what this brother does for Christ now. Thank you, Lord!)

I hung these pictures all over my wall. I dressed like Madonna in my room and wildly danced around to songs like "Material Girl" and "Dress You Up," perceiving that it would either be luck or power that would win me the attention of an attractive and seemingly successful man. I even played the Dream Date board game, where my friends and I would compete for the pictures of the hunks on various cards and their incredibly unrealistic descriptions on the back. I was trained to "win" a worthwhile man, and sex seemed to provide that hidden power. So if someone desired sex with me, it equaled power and, ultimately, success, in my mind.

This distorted thinking led to my kissing boys at the age of eleven and being sexually active by seventeen. These were all by my choice; I was not forced into anything. I realize there are women who have had much more traumatic stories and who engaged in sexual conduct much younger than I did. My emphasis here is not on the age as much as it is the distorted belief that this was right and good.

I also over-romanticized every interaction because I believed that affection signified commitment. Every boy became the one I would marry. And while I was not promiscuous without the feelings of "love," I was in love with love, or "boy crazy." I would justify my early sexual interaction because I thought it confirmed that mutual passion would hold us together for life. How very foolish I was. I had no idea of God's view of my body or how precious it was to Him.

I lived based entirely on feelings and my own understanding of love for the first three decades of my life. I genuinely thought that as long as I was following my heart, things would turn out right. But for a woman as passionate as I am, this led to danger and ultimately to disaster, no matter how I tried to spin it. During my darkest days, included in the five-year span of this testimony, the culmination of these choices came together, and I faced divorce, financial bankruptcy, a bitter custody battle, a significant breakdown in health, and a period of secretive homosexual sin. I was a living example of Proverbs 19:3: "A person's own folly leads to their ruin, yet their heart rages against the LORD."

In hindsight, I realize that having previously associated physical affection with love and power, the absence of it after my divorce left me feeling unloved and powerless. Additionally, by this time I had become so self-centered that I incorrectly placed all the blame of my failed marriage on my ex-husband. I was angry and bitter. I was desperately looking for the desire and longing of my soul to be filled at almost any cost. Finding God was the last thing I expected.

I got saved on a dark night in 2012 when I accepted Jesus Christ as my Lord and Savior. My consecration began, but it was slow and painful because of the way I struggled to make sense of the call to follow Christ in a new life. When I became a believer, the idea that I was supposed to abstain from sex until marriage (or remarriage, in my case) left me angry, incorrectly perceiving that God was punishing me instead of providing for me—as though He were taking and not giving. I didn't even see the possibility of changing my opinions about premarital sex. I had a distorted and worldly view that had been long ingrained.

My ideas of what I wanted to do with my newfound freedom conflicted with the calling that I knew I was receiving from God to live a different life. My previous understanding of how to live was revealing a stark contrast compared with what I was learning from the Scriptures in my new Christian walk. I was being pressed to grow and learn a new perspective. I knew that if I were granted God's understanding in this area, it was likely not going to match my previous plans. Yet I couldn't ignore the Holy Spirit prompting me to learn the boundaries of holy living.

Eventually, the difficulty of trying to navigate both worlds became too heavy. And one night in my lonely bedroom, angry and desperate for an answer, I finally got the courage to ask in boldness. On this night I also understood the call to write this book.

I don't want to paint a false picture. This was not some holy image of me sitting in a church pew, in a nice church-proper dress, where God answered me by divine inspiration in a hymnal. I was an angry woman wearing purposefully provocative clothes (even though I was by myself) in flesh that was hungry and restless and consumed with craving. I was completely self-absorbed, focused on all I perceived I was lacking, and it was driving me out of my mind. I wasn't coming to God to welcome His presence on holy ground; I was demanding that He answer me in my lust and self-absorption. I wanted to know—demanded to know—if I truly loved someone and wanted to give them my body, why wasn't it okay for me to do so as an act of love toward them? And in my passion, my incredible Savior mercifully allowed me to hear clearly what I know didn't come from me.

He answered, "Because your body is so priceless, so important to Me that I don't want anyone else to have it unless they promise Me that they will love you forever."

This answer came not as an audible voice that someone else could have heard if they had been in the same room, but as a clearly distinguishable message inside that was meant for me. This was not a thought or inner voice like we sometimes conjure up on our own. It wasn't like that at all. And this was certainly not the way I was thinking or even could have imagined thinking. I believed that this answer came from God, and it stopped me in my tracks. The importance of this message was one I knew needed to be shared with others—with you—when the time was right.

I've learned that when we truly want to learn how to follow Him, He will place resources in our path to support that pursuit. While His Word is always perfect in that instruction, I began to watch as He ushered in several other believers to help me connect my flawed thinking of the past to the consequences I experienced. Early in my new walk with Christ, a Christian mentor was the first to rebuke my practice of walking by feelings instead of by faith. She pointed me to Jeremiah 17:9, which says that the heart is wicked and deceitful. While I distinctly remember feeling defensive at the time and thinking she didn't understand that I had good intentions by following my heart, God has since shown me that He put her there in my life for this important lesson. She was the first to explain—courageously and in love—the disastrous effects of following my heart. And having faced such disaster, I finally understood that my thinking was indeed flawed and entirely self-focused.

One of my pastors, James Betner, once said, "Feelings are like traffic lights. Stay there long enough, and they'll change." I heard this statement early on in my new life and was genuinely dumbfounded by it at first. In reflection, I realized I had tested and proved this statement true many times over. When my feelings changed, that was when disaster set in. It was more and more proof of my flawed and distorted thinking that I had been used to living with. Pastor Betner also became the first person that I shared with "publicly" (in confidence) the secret of my homosexual sin. I thank God for his clear rebuke and the courage he had on that day to speak to me of a life I could have only dreamed of—the one I doubted, the one God was calling me to, the one I am living now.

Yet despite all these connections and seeds being planted, my strong feelings did not just die off. Time and time again, my feelings led to difficult choices. While I'm nowhere near perfected, I can confirm that submitting my emotions and passion under the authority of Jesus Christ has paved the foundation for the transformation that has taken place. It is my hope to inspire another passionate sister to the same transformation.

With that hope, I have asked God how He wants to use my voice, and I believe it is to reveal from a woman's perspective the "before" and "after" of what it means to live for the passion of the world and what it means to live instead for the passion of Jesus. I have tried to include critical parts of my testimony in each chapter, along with the instruction that God taught me directly relating to those times. My story is ultimately one of dying to self, and for me, that meant crucifying my worldly passion and handing it to the only One worthy of it.

I have been prayerful to put together what I believe is a balance of full disclosure and God-honoring testimony. It is not my intent in this book to dishonor anyone who has been a part of my story. Each has played an important role. I have asked others to review, double-check, and rebuke anything that they have seen that does not fit that criteria. It is my desire to have handled well the Word and truth of Jesus Christ, and I take this responsibility seriously. My mission is that you, reader, might hear of the mighty power of our Savior through my small voice.

While this book is not intended for a young audience, I imagine it may reach those even in their early teens. I pray that the sexually focused content does not lead anyone astray, but instead creates in the reader an undeniable urge to pursue God's path for her life. Those who I think may be most impacted are women in their twenties, thirties, forties, and maybe fifties, especially those who are single or separated. I'm specifically writing to those sisters out there who, like me, just simply don't know how to balance the calling of holiness with an intense and fiery passion inside.

To those cherished sisters specifically, I ask you to please not read this intending to find all your own answers here. I remember doing that myself. I'd pick up someone else's story to see how they did it, only to be left somewhat disappointed, wanting more when their book ended and my situation continued. I need you to know that my book will never be enough. God's Word will be. His grace is sufficient (2 Cor. 12:9). It is my intention to present here the answers I found to be aligned with the Word of God for my life. Your conduct should be determined by your personal relationship with Jesus Christ and what is represented in Scripture. It is the user manual for our human condition.

It's my hope that, for those who have known me my whole life and have been confused or conflicted about the dramatic change they've seen in me, this may provide some explanation of my new behavior. I ask grace and forgiveness from those I have hurt along the way as I tried to take new steps in a new life. Please know that I never could have predicted my life to be as it is now. I did not plan or seek the change, but I know it's real because it happened despite myself.

I give thanks to God, ultimately, for paying through His Son the price for my sin that I could never have paid myself. I'm still learning just how unworthy I am of that gift.

I thank my husband, Geoff, who acts as the physical manifestation of God's unconditional love for me each day. Being your wife is the honor of my life next to being His daughter. Thank you for being strong enough to stand by faithfully as God uses my ugliness to show His grace upon us all.

I thank my beloved children—Aidan, Andre, and Madeo—for allowing me to guard, guide, and pray for them as long as I am able.

I thank my truest sisters in Christ who have loved at all times (Prov. 17:17), and my parents who have done their best with me despite me. Thank you for always trying to steer my ship among the wild waves.

I thank my incredible editors for the gift of godly rebuke and correction, my peer reviewers for their honest feedback and wise counsel, and to all of those who have been instrumental in helping to bring to fruition that which I am still scared to give the world.

> Come and hear, all you who fear God, and I will declare what He has done for my soul.
> (Ps. 66:16 NKJV)

Joanna

CHAPTER 1

Burnt Offering: From Rebellion to Submission

You will seek Me and find Me when you search for
Me with all your heart.
(Jer. 29:13 NASB)

It was April 1, 2012, and I found myself waking up on my friend's couch in New Jersey. Less than twenty-four hours before, I was married, living in my own home—a house that I called my "realistic dream home"—and sleeping (even if it was lonely) in a king-sized bed in a warm cherrywood bedroom. My bedroom had a window that the sun would magically filter through in the morning in small gentle rays, like in a Disney movie. It was the peaceful part of our home—a reminder of life on the outside.

My two-and-a-half-year-old son now lay next to me on my friend's couch.

There were nine of us in the house. And four pets. The old dog urinated on the floor frequently. Most of the time we shared one bathroom because the one upstairs didn't work well and the teenagers mostly used it, which made it unbearably gross. Although this could have been a jovial sleepover party with my friend and her kids, it was more like the worst hangover of my life. The day before, I had come home to the catalyst that convinced me I had to leave my husband. I took a small amount of clothes for myself and my son, my dad's guitar, my phone, and my makeup. The police helped me get in the black minivan that my friend drove to come pick me up.

I ended the lie that was our "happy marriage" and our life together—and the abuse. I knew I would not go back. Part of me was relieved and excited to restart life, convinced that *I could do it!* As a single mom, the shocking reality of the responsibility, the unknown loneliness ahead, and the financial weight sat next to me that morning but didn't speak a word. I was glad it didn't speak. I didn't intend to listen anyway. I intended to be an immediate success story like all the songs I would play on repeat during this time, celebrating and touting independence with themes of resiliency, and even "sparkling" like the strong woman I believed I was. I was determined to sparkle and not acknowledge the clouds growing more and more dense in the sky above.

And so for a while, I did. I sparkled with what I now know was false hope based on my own potential. I hit the unhealthiest weight of my life at a size zero and was happy that I felt skinny for once and looked like I had wanted to look in a bikini. I bought an electronic cigarette in cool menthol. It was safe to be around my son, they said; it only gave off water vapor. I "did me" because now I could.

The divorce took fourteen months. During this time, I burned many things around me—most impactfully, my soul. I made many mistakes as I searched and searched for that which would potentially satisfy and heal me. But something would emerge through the ashes like the occasional ray that had gently filtered through my bedroom window from the outside. It was there even on the days I stayed in bed all day in my darkened dining-room-turned-bedroom, refusing to acknowledge it. The winds of change, as they say, were blowing.

In one of the most important statements of my life, my friend and her husband put forth the condition that my son and I could stay in their house, rent-free, for as long as we needed to, provided that I committed to going to church.

If I didn't do it on the outside, I certainly had an inward eye roll at what seemed like an unnecessary and rather dramatic requirement. The alternative was to pay rent and, worse, harm the relationship. Despite the chaos, I wanted to stay. So I put on my Sunday best to hide my rebellious spirit and proceeded to church.

The church I attended growing up was always systematic, structured, controlled, and most of the time, anything but passionate except when they talked about money. Later, when I transferred to another church, it was a lighter version of this with the occasional hint of passion filtering through. I was never drawn to the rituals of church or the people that I saw in it who seemed to be anything but passionate about what they claimed. And because I wasn't reading the Bible, I didn't have an accurate idea of God's love for me.

I knew Jesus was a real man, and I think I believed He was God incarnate, but I did not recognize the value in living by His commands or studying His Word. The Bible had always seemed like an outdated set of rules that maybe applied to priests or nuns trying to live a life of service to the church. Since I didn't fit that mold, there didn't seem to be value in reading it. Jesus, God the Father, and the Holy Spirit seemed like untouchable figures with a million layers of people I'd have to go through to even come close to them, people like the nuns and priests I perceived to be living a much holier life than

I was. I now know that my perception of those servant lifestyles was religious. I was mistakenly associating ritual and sacrifice with the ability to claim a real relationship with God. Because I did not participate in religion, I did not believe I was qualified to participate in relationship.

Yet the pastor I encountered by my friend's important ultimatum was entirely different from the nuns and priests I had previously met. Pastor James was a real man who had lived a real life, which he colorfully inserted into his sermons each week to show just how far God had brought him. He was beyond passionate, yet calm. Bold to the point of almost being rude, he was always confident and truthful. He was clearly a dedicated servant of God, yet he hadn't grown up in some monastery. He hadn't been serving as an altar boy in some church when he was confirmed into ministry. He was living real life and making real mistakes when God claimed his heart and changed his life. His stories were amazing. And his words knocked the wind out of me on several occasions as he showed the direct correlation of what God had done in his life to that which was in the Bible. I was mesmerized as I listened to him—and it was starting to impact me beyond the pew.

I'm not sure I can describe tangibly what it was that started to change, but I know that my mind and my heart kept lingering and mulling over things the pastor had said well beyond the time that I left church. This wasn't fitting my check-the-box plan I had originally intended when I agreed to go to church weekly. I didn't know what was happening, and honestly, I didn't want anything to happen; I had enough to deal with. I didn't recognize that it was God's Word starting to cut as a two-edged sword. My sparkle started to feel more like a conduit attracting lightning I couldn't handle. A different burn. I hated it, but at the same time knew deeply that it was necessary.

The proof of the death occurring in me was emerging instead of the sparkle effect I had wanted, and it felt like the waves were rising well above my head. As I sat in church each week and listened to the sermons, conviction rained down from those previously looming clouds above, and I cried and I cried until I could barely come up from the water. Not for just one day, but many. I know that those who observed me were likely convinced I was having a nervous breakdown. And externally, I tried to fight it with everything I had. I wanted to thrive and shine like I claimed I was going to do. Yet I couldn't deny that I was beginning to crave the same passion I saw my pastor speak with. I wanted to understand how this man whom I heard could be so outspoken about his love affair with the man Jesus Christ.

While I wasn't a born-again believer at this point, I started to read the Bible—not just in church but at home on my own. I started to wonder if there was something in there that actually related to me and my circumstances the way it did for Pastor James. I started to wonder if something in there could explain the consistent passion in me that seemed like an unquenchable and untamable fire. I was looking for these answers as well as direction in my difficult circumstances, which included the divorce, custody battle, secret sexual sin, and future living arrangements for my son and myself. These major issues seemed way too heavy to figure out on my own, and I had previously depended on everyone else around me for answers. My paradigm was shifting.

I slowly started to go to Him in prayer instead of to those around me for their advice. Quite honestly, despite their good intentions, no one could really understand what was going on in me. I didn't even understand that I was slowly dying to self, against all my original wishes. Trying to find God was not something I was imagining or comforting myself with in the midst of a breakdown. While some days were quiet, like Sabbath rest, many more felt like my heart and my passions were being burned by acid and their healing redirected to a place I had never known. It was an intense period of breaking and building, and I was diligent in fighting it.

One night, at the height of my battle, I submitted my life and my heart under the authority of Jesus Christ and accepted Him as my Lord and Savior. Isaiah 42:25 exemplifies the state I had succumbed to in order to get to this point: "They were enveloped in flames, but they still refused to understand. They were consumed by fire, but they did not learn their lesson" (Isa. 42:25 NLT).

This is by far the hardest part to write because I have three young boys who will someday read this book. There are other loved ones who will read this, perhaps having witnessed my outward state slowly falling apart but not being able to connect it with the true internal struggle that would have explained what they saw. Others will read this who will wish me all the harm I knowingly and unknowingly inflicted on them by my dark behavior. To all those mentioned here, I ask for your unjustified grace and forgiveness.

This is the darkest part of my testimony. But I stand firm on God's Word, which tells me that we shall overcome by the blood of the Lamb and the word of our testimony (Rev. 12:11), so I believe that not only will I continue to overcome but that someone else may be inspired to as well. The darkest hour is before the dawn. While my testimony has been woven specifically through places in this book, it's here that I want to convey the depth and the darkness that were a result of my choice for sexual sin.

MY DARK NIGHT OF SUBMISSION

I packed a bag for the weekend and drove twenty-five minutes away to my cousin's house. My cousin was single at the time and had a beautiful, modern house in the same suburb I always said I wanted to live in when I was growing up. My son was away for the weekend with his dad. My cousin had gone somewhere to have fun. I came to her house, alone, for a retreat.

Compared to the cramped, chaotic quarters where I was used to living, her house felt so big and almost annoyingly quiet. I was sure to bring alcohol to help me deal with it, even though I knew my cousin said I could help myself to anything she had. I brought my Bible as well, but only in an angry show of rebellion; I imagined bringing it and not reading it like I said I would.

I walked around the house considering what I would do next: order some takeout and not share it with anyone (and not have to explain why) . . . lounge on the giant couch with the remote all to myself . . . watch movies and drink whatever I wanted. *After all, it could be worse,* I thought. I wasn't out hanging around in some bar or driving home when I shouldn't be driving.

Now I would like to clarify that at no time in this process, thanks be to God, did I ever have an addiction to alcohol. But knowing that I've always been a lightweight, it didn't take much for me to get a "buzz" safely in my home during some dark moments. In this particular instance, though, I was more than happy to find something to help numb me.

That being said, what I really wanted to do, I wasn't doing. I wanted the temporary fix of the sexual sin I felt like I couldn't live without. I wanted it so badly that I was getting uglier and uglier in my schemes to get it—even though I knew that what I was chasing was never going to be mine and wasn't meant to be. As many times as I felt entirely fulfilled by the sin, as if I had been waiting my whole life for it, it gave only fleeting satisfaction that actually left a bigger hole in me than I had ever experienced before. I was burning, yet willingly fanning the flames. At this point the burn was raging so fiercely in my mind that I didn't even need to engage in illicit sexual behavior to be consumed by my desires.

With the alcohol starting to take over, I walked around the house with a maddening passion rising within me. My heart racing, my pulse too fast, I wanted to reach for the phone and tell her she needed to get here. I needed a fix to calm the storm, or something really bad was going to happen. She would be worried, and that might be enough to get her here. The house was becoming deafeningly quiet, so I turned the TV up and took another drink while I paced.

I walked by the kitchen table, angry to see the pink-covered Bible inside my bag. But what was *that* going to do to save me from myself? To me, it was a book of judgmental, outdated, man-written nonsense. Why would I even consider living by something that a man wrote "a million years" ago? In my hostile state, I actually wanted to prove it wrong. After all, my friend had claimed that every topic and problem was referenced in the Bible, but I knew it wouldn't address what I was feeling. I was convinced that no one knew what I was feeling, and I didn't want to live without this passion, even if it was killing me. Even if.

To prove the Bible wrong, I opened it randomly to the Song of Solomon (also called Song of Songs), although I didn't know the name of the book then. At that time, I was unfamiliar with the books of the Bible, and the only thing that made sense to me were the page numbers. A phrase like "Mark six-fourteen" was just a meaningless jumble of names and numbers. It all sounded rather outdated, exactly as I had expected, with *thee* and *thou* in the middle of sentences. But I lingered a few seconds longer than I expected to as some of it also sounded passionate and needy. Perhaps there were some sexual overtones in it? The verse "Tell him I am faint with love" (Song 5:8) sounded a little more like someone I could relate to. But I was maddened with "love," and this Scripture passage seemed tame compared to my passion. I slammed the Bible closed and left it on the table as I tried to process the steadily increasing emotion rising within me, and all that had led me to this point.

While I didn't know it at the time, my sexual interaction with this woman was damaging me deeply, as the Scripture confirms it to be unnatural sexual sin against one's own body (Rom. 1:26; 1 Cor. 6:18). In the process of the downward spiral that had emerged, I also found myself coveting, lying, worshiping a false god, unintentionally hurting others, and encouraging infidelity. Somehow, this one-time supposedly fun, innocent deviation of pleasure had led me to committing most of the sins warned against in the Ten Commandments. Still, in my denial, I considered myself a good person (contradicting Romans 3:10). I didn't actually consider myself drenched in sin. I was following my heart and was blinded by ungodly desire.

I didn't want to hurt anyone, and I really did think I was acting out of love. Although I earlier referred to my initial act as intended to be a one-time fun deviation, I thought I was deeply in love with the one who engaged in it with me. Ours had been a long friendship with many intricately intertwined roots. This was not a college experiment. It was a misdirected and selfish counterfeit "love" that, in fact, was ruining the deepest parts of our beings and what we liked most about each other.

It was even more maddening because I believed I had started from a place of genuine love but couldn't understand why my life was being laid waste before me. But the "love" had turned to addiction—and addiction demands satisfaction. Addiction will burn and consume anything to satisfy itself, even to the point of destroying the person held in its vicelike grip. The sin against one's own body is distinct because it is a sin that can destroy the very home in which it resides. And even if it doesn't completely destroy its home, it leaves a lingering, overpowering stench like the smell of smoke long after something has burned.

I couldn't deny it. I had made too many mistakes somehow on the road that I believed to be the right one. This had all gone too far. So that night I drank. And I examined my cousin's medicine cabinet to consider what would be enough to finish me. It could be a glorious plunge into the flames of my desire. Weren't romance novels written like that—with lovers dying for love? I would leave a statement of just how strong my love had become. No one would forget, especially since they wouldn't know for days.

My son. Three years old. I couldn't think of him. That would stop me. But was I even worthy of being his mother? What did I know of love? How would I teach him how to have a healthy relationship? All my own choices were quickly proving to be drastically wrong.

I stumbled up the stairs toward the bedroom. There was one bedroom, entirely empty except for a lamp and a mattress, both on the floor. In hindsight, I don't know why (and I don't remember doing it), but I stumbled upstairs carrying the pink Bible. The anguished cries flowed from my heart and the tears from my eyes so intensely that I just couldn't stand the pain. I didn't know if it was more painful to keep them in or let them come out. I fell to the floor, pounded the mattress with my hand, and collapsed on it in a drunken, desperate state, where I think I continued to cry in my sleep.

I don't know how much time passed, but when I woke, I sensed an incredible darkness even before my eyes opened. No light had been turned on. I opened my eyes, and as I did so, it felt like a knife went through my open left eye. I screamed and threw my hands over it. The pain was the sharp stab of my cornea being ripped, as it had before when my son had accidentally pushed his tiny fingernail into the same eye six months earlier. The doctor said it had entirely healed. But this was brand-new. And this time, there was nothing there to scratch my eye as his little finger had in the previous injury.

If you've never had an eye injury, perhaps you would assume, like I did, that you would at least have vision in the uninjured eye, but this isn't the case. Both eyes naturally try to open, and even though you keep the injured one shut, the effort of the other trying to open creates stress on the injured one as it tries not to. I continued to scream into the empty room for no one to hear. The pain was excruciating, and tears started to flow heavily due to my anguish and desperate frustration. The salt from the tears seeped into the rip in my eye and escalated the pain until it was nearly unbearable.

Holding my hand over my left eye, I frantically searched around the mattress and floor for my phone. I would call for help. But there was no phone to be found anywhere, even though I was certain I had brought it into the room with me. I searched for the lamp to turn it on, only to realize by feeling the cord that it wasn't plugged in, and I wasn't about to search the wall with my fingers to find the outlet. There was a bathroom across the hall, but I didn't even know if I could get there. The confusion, anger, and deep pain became immobilizing.

As I groped around the floor with my hand and touched what I realized was the pink-covered Bible, I immediately felt mocked. If this God cared so much about me, why would He be doing this to me? Why would He put me in a room with nothing, in an empty house, in a painful stupor (all while going through divorce, bankruptcy, and an awful custody battle), having lost the very house I loved so much and the life I thought was mine, only to covet another relationship that I couldn't and wouldn't have, but felt like I needed—and now He would take my eyesight as well? A loving God wouldn't do this! He would have protected me, saved me from this, saved me from myself, but instead He was mocking me, still claiming to be right at my very darkest hour.

I opened the Bible passionately, angrily, and tried, holding my left eye, to read something, anything, on the random page with my teary uninjured eye. Despite the darkness, the moment my eye met the page, I was unexplainably able to make out the slightest of words, and the rage in me boiled over. I grasped the pink-covered Bible, screamed with everything in me, and threw it at the wall, breaking the binding and sending a crash throughout the house with the echo of my enraged scream, "You win!" Somewhat shocked, yet once more drowning in despair, I proclaimed out loud, "I give up," and collapsed in the middle of the room on the dark floor holding my hand over my weeping eye.

When I woke, it was daylight, but my night wasn't over. Something had changed, however. I would still choose darkness a bit longer, but it no longer held the same appeal it had before. Although I was still in this big house by myself, now I didn't feel entirely alone in the room. It was as though someone sat there with me, silently watching me as if I were in a hospital bed and them quietly observing for signs of life.

I found my pink Bible, its hard binding hanging by a thread or two on the glued paper backing that held the pages together. Looking at it now, I no longer felt mocked. It seemed in its present state like something I could relate to. I held my left eye shut, and I sat on the floor and read. I really didn't know what I was reading, and I'm not sure it even made sense to me at the time. But something about it was comforting and necessary. By the afternoon my eye was healed enough to drive. I got in my car, bag and Bible in hand, and left the big house.

LIFE AFTER THE DEATH OF SEXUAL SIN

> You have been chosen to know me, believe in me,
> and understand that I alone am God.
> (Isa. 43:10 NLT)

When I consider what my God did for me that night—as I now write it years later from the perspective of a life rebuilt—I hardly can grasp the miracle personally intended for me. If not for the grace of God, I wouldn't have survived my many selfish decisions. Much processing has taken place to allow me to understand the importance of my submission to the Lord.

In hindsight, I realize that my obsession with "love" led me to associate it with death. Ironically, I realize that I was waiting for someone to love me enough to be willing to die for me. Isn't that the theme of the most passionate love songs and movies? In the greatest love stories, like *Romeo and Juliet,* people die for their love. So maybe if I died for love, someone would understand how much I loved. And if someone wasn't willing to die for my love, then they probably weren't the right one for me. I was "in love with love," and I felt like I had been born this way.

I found that to be accurate, but not in the way I originally perceived it.

God had created me to desire Him from my innermost being. All the passion I had been seeking from another person was exactly what He provided for me. He took the beatings, the accusations, the nails, and the undeserved death to ensure that one day we would be reunited for eternity. He had already offered exactly what I had been searching for my whole life in another person. He was just waiting humbly for me to see it. In my search, when I was desperate enough to think I had to die for it myself, He brought me out, but not without evidence.

Unlike the account in the third chapter of Daniel in which Shadrach, Meshach, and Abednego were thrown into the fiery furnace but came out without even their clothes smelling of smoke, I came out as nothing less than a visibly burnt offering. I didn't go into the furnace with great faith as these men did. I went in because of my desire for pleasure in pursuit of a foreign god. I walked myself into the furnace after it. Instead of letting me stay and truly understand the full consequence of my sin, God actually went before me into it with the appropriate tools. He entered into the middle of it with me as He promised He would, confirmed the claim that I was His even before my life began, and then He made good on these promises with a grand rescue (Rom. 6:23; Deut. 31:8; Psa. 23:4; Eph. 1:4–5).

> But the Lord has taken you and brought you out of the iron furnace, out of Egypt, to be His people, an inheritance, as you are this day.
> (Deut. 4:20 NKJV)

The smell of smoke still permeates my clothes to remind me of where I've been, of where He found me. To me, it's a pleasing aroma, a beautiful reminder of the living sacrifice He created me to be for Him and of the truth I've discovered.

> First I predicted your rescue, then I saved you and proclaimed it to the world. No foreign god has ever done this.
> (Isa. 43:12 NLT)

Contrary to everything I had been saying and feeling, the God who loved me *was* saving me. I was waiting for Him to prove Himself to me, but I can confirm that on that dark night His presence was palpable and as real as anything I have ever experienced.

Psalm 23:4 states, "Even though I walk through the darkest valley, I will fear no evil, for you are with me; your rod and your staff, they comfort me." This verse didn't make sense before I got saved. I considered a blanket and food to be more comforting than a rod or staff! Weren't those used as weapons or instruments for discipline?

I have since learned that the rod was actually an instrument of authority and was used by shepherds for counting, guiding, rescuing, and protecting their sheep. The staff was an instrument of support. My God was showing up in all authority as the One to claim me, rescue me, and protect me from my own choices. He waited until those choices brought me to my knees so I could understand the painful consequences of those decisions. Much like Paul on the road to Damascus, He needed to strip me of self-sufficiency, even removing my eyesight, so I could see Him. And then He made sure to show up with the appropriate instruments for the dark. The rescue was just the beginning though.

Unlike some fantastic stories of instant-healing miracles that we hear, I was not an immediate success story. I want to be clear that I was not then and am not today completely cured of my sinful desires. As long as we are in this life, we will battle our sin nature. That sin nature will not be removed until we join the Savior in a sin-free eternity. In the meantime, I've learned the necessity of relying on the power of intervention and redemption in the name and person of Jesus Christ.

Even as I fully came to accept my forgiveness in Christ, I still experienced the lasting painful effects of my sin. The particular sin that controlled me at the time has become more disdainful and less appealing to me as time has passed, but to this day I'm still haunted by memories of what I what once considered pleasure. In talking with others who have come out of this dark place, I know their stories to be similar as well. Even as a "burnt offering," by refraining from sexual sin I was becoming a living sacrifice (Rom. 12:1). But I once heard a pastor say that the problem with a living sacrifice is that it often wants to crawl off the altar. Indeed, there were days that I did just that as I struggled to accept that fulfillment could come without sex to make me feel loved and satisfied.

I suffered from the initial emptiness I felt, the intensified desire to be pulled back into a false comfort zone, the fear that I would never be fulfilled or satisfied again, and my constant question about what label applied to me. Was I a homosexual? A recovering sex addict? Was I bisexual? Could I just play it off like a college experiment, even though I knew it was much more than that? I've since come to understand the importance of refraining from labeling ourselves as anything other than "in Christ." (More on that in the chapter "Exchanging the Natural.")

I also had to face the harsh reality that if I were eventually going to be in a lifelong intimate relationship in the future, I would have to disclose this portion of my past. What would he think about me? Would he be able to trust that I wouldn't go back into the same sin? Would I be able to trust that I wouldn't? Wouldn't that make even the best possible man run?

I eventually even came up with a lighter version of the story that I could tell. But in one instance, a man whom I briefly dated threatened to tell my church about my secret and shame me. Carrying all these hardships, questions, and deep burdens, I was overwhelmed during the times I didn't seek and hold fast to my true identity in God. Thankfully, Scripture was my constant reassurance. I clung to it with each of these hurdles. It was and is still my lifeline.

I found great hope in God's Word when I read, "If anyone is in Christ, he is a new creation; old things have passed away; behold, all things have become new" (2 Cor. 5:17 NKJV). I was slowly grasping that this verse doesn't say that a void would be left. It actually says that new (and much better) things would replace the old things. In fact, the preceding verse says, "Even though we have known Christ according to the flesh, yet now we know Him thus no longer" (2 Cor. 5:16 NKJV). I started to fully believe that He was not only going to do something new in my life, but He was going to teach me a whole different way of understanding and knowing His love—not through the flesh, which I had mistakenly thought was the source of true love, but through the Spirit.

As a born-again believer diligently pursuing the Word, a new and healthier life was steadily emerging. The Holy Spirit took up residence in my heart and started to change the way I wanted to conduct my life. While the burden wasn't entirely released because of the tug-of-war with my sin nature, which tried to hold on to the past, the weight became more manageable the more I submitted. I started to actually try to live as the Bible taught and love as Jesus loved. I began to see value in serving others again, and once I began to take my focus off myself and all my problems, I became healthier. The sexual sin I was involved with became less and less fitting to my new walk with Jesus, and He began to put new desires into my heart. He planted seeds in me to want to seek out the path toward a Christian marriage.

Confirmed as His, I sought the specific action steps I would need take to walk in submission to Him and resist the pull that was still trying to undermine me. So while one hand was wiping my tears, my other hand took His hand to depend on Him for strength. I'm writing this today because He made a way—and He can for you too. I might have walked out of that fire as a burnt offering, but I walked out with Him and toward Him and into an undeserved new life.

> I want you to know me more than I want burnt offerings.
> (Hos. 6:6 NLT)

CHAPTER 2

Why on Earth Would I Pursue Sexual Purity? A View from Earth and Heaven

Be holy, because I am holy.
(1 Peter 1:16)

I had to survive a massive culmination of my own sinful choices before I was inspired to learn the value of pursuing sexual purity. My hope is that you have not had to do so, yet I also realize that you may think the information in this chapter is somewhat obvious. If you're tempted to skip over this chapter, that's understandable. After all, if you've ever had a family health class in school or had "the talk" with your parents, you probably have some idea of the benefits of remaining sexually pure. I had heard all the worldly reasons also. But it may help to hear about the other benefits that those classes and most parental talks don't discuss: the holy benefits. I had to learn them the hard way.

The importance of this short chapter is that it's the "why" of the message of the book. It is intended to inspire a path toward sexual purity that ultimately reflects submission to the Lord. The points covered here provided a foundation for my decision to follow God's path instead of my own.

THE VIEW FROM EARTH

Even from a secular standpoint, there are many valid reasons to abstain from sex until marriage. For example, abstinence will prevent:

- Unplanned pregnancy
- Sexually transmitted diseases (STDs) such as HIV, AIDS, and cervical cancer caused by HPV
- Emotional complications in a relationship due to premarital sex
- Regret from sexual interaction without commitment
- Sex from becoming a false barometer of the health of your relationship

All of these are good reasons in themselves for avoiding sex before marriage. Plenty of studies have shown that significant chemical changes occur in our bodies when we engage in sexual conduct. No matter how much anyone tries to not involve their heart, there is no option for avoiding the physical effects of sex that literally alter our brains. It is the reason for the common reference to rose-colored glasses that people often use to imply a distortion to someone's ability to appropriately discern the health of a relationship once sex has been initiated outside of marriage. Sex changes things. Those changes are meant to bond husband and wife in their marriage—never to benefit those outside of this sacred relationship. I have learned that in my own personal journey. While this book is not intended to present a comprehensive scientific explanation of the dramatic impact sexual activity has on us, I do urge you to look at the array of established and credible research that has confirmed it.

While that may be the science of why you should avoid sex before marriage, it's important to keep in mind that science doesn't contradict God, because God is the source of truth. Science is simply the explanation for the physical laws and consequences that He has set in place. So yes, these are the "worldly" reasons for not engaging in premarital sex, but it's more important to understand that they align with God's purposes. The consequences that are prevented by abstaining from sex outside of marriage are simply another way for God to show that you will be blessed if you do things His way.

The View from Heaven

Here is where I want to share with you how my understanding about purity began to shift from a temporal, worldly perspective to an eternal, holy perspective. Although we will never be 100 percent pure ourselves until we reach heaven, we are all called in this life to pursue holiness completely, which includes the pursuit of sexual purity. The grace of Jesus Christ is that His sacrifice has covered where we have fallen and will continue to fall short. Our hearts, though, should yearn for victory, so it is important to understand what victory looks like as viewed from heaven.

As I have previously shared, it wasn't until I got saved and accepted Jesus as my Lord and Savior that I began to connect with the command of sexual purity. I had to suffer a lot before I understood the benefit from God's perspective. At first, I didn't understand it at all. Eventually my flesh and heart calmed once I began to believe that God's plan for me to enjoy sex as He created it to be was the better plan. As I continued to seek out His Word for answers, I started to understand why the call of purity was important to God and why it should be important to me:

- Purity is a command, and our obedience is a display of our love to Him (Ex. 20:14; Matt. 5:28; John 14:15).
- Purity enables us to acknowledge the Creator (God) above the created (sex) and, therefore, to also be a witness to others (Col. 3:5).
- Purity prepares us to receive the good and perfect gift of sex within His holy timing for us (James 1:17; Eccl. 3:11).
- Purity protects us from the consequences of sexual immorality (1 Cor. 7:1–4).
- Purity helps to maintain our credibility, reputation, and value as someone to be trusted, not led by emotion, temptation, or manipulation (Mark 7:20–23; Eph. 5:3).
- Purity prepares us for holy, not tainted, oneness with another person, bonded by love and not by the shackles of sin (1 Cor. 6:16–17).
- Purity sought together helps us understand the depth of commitment our future spouse also professes in his duty to the Lord Jesus Christ (Eccl. 12:13–14).
- Purity is an intentional means for us to be holy because He is holy (1 Peter 1:16).

The view from heaven reveals that God doesn't intend for physical affection to be the means to love. God is love. *He* is the source of that. God views sex as a gift to be enjoyed between husband and wife, once confirmed by a holy commitment to Him. It is an expression of not only His good gifts toward us, but also His plan to protect us from difficult consequences.

Remember what I heard God answer me when I asked Him why I couldn't have premarital sex? "Because your body is so priceless, so important to Me, that I don't want anyone else to have it unless they promise Me that they will love you forever."

God was telling me that He intended to hold anyone who engaged in sex with me accountable as though they were promising Him to make a lifetime commitment to me. My earlier belief that physical affection signified a lifetime commitment wasn't actually completely off. It was just missing the presence and authority of the One who not only gives sex as a good gift, but also ensures the accountability of its use. God wanted for me the fulfillment and satisfaction I had wanted as well (although I had misinterpreted it through my distorted human viewpoint). But He actually had the means to provide the fulfillment. I had no ability to find on my own a gift only He could provide. I grossly misunderstood the origin and intention of sex and physical affection: it wasn't a strategy; it wasn't a barometer. It was a celebration.

The view from heaven is simply this: You are precious enough for Jesus to die for, and He is not going to concede to you having anything other than His good and perfect gift. He is watching from heaven as He continues to prepare a place for you. You are His bride, and He's not going to let just anyone have you while you're here.

God is telling you that you are not for sale. He may give you as a temporary gift to a man for the duration of your life together, but He wants to ensure that man fears Him, knows to whom you actually belong, and knows he should commit his actions to God.

Without God's view—the view from heaven—we simply can't make this judgment on our own. God is the One who sees the heart (1 Sam. 16:7), so He should be the One to tell you whom you should marry and enjoy this gift with. Your heavenly Daddy needs to give you His approval because He's the only One who has the correct view—the only view that matters.

This does not mean that you will marry a sinless man, but it means that you should marry a God-fearing man who is prepared to give a good answer when Jesus asks him what he did with his wife. That man is going to be held accountable for how he's received and treated you. And you, sister, are going to be held to the same account.

The view from heaven is that God sees your husband as the same precious gift He has seen and confirmed in you. God only wants the very best woman for your husband, and you are being called to that same level of responsibility and accountability. And the view from heaven is how good it is when we extend our submissive hands to receive the gifts that are good and perfect from above (James 1:17). When you willingly accept that, you accept God's gift of experiencing one of the closest things to heaven that we have on this earth.

Why on earth would you pursue sexual purity? Because any choice for purity and holiness is the absolute best thing we can experience this side of heaven.

CHAPTER 3

Surveying the Landscape: An Honest View of the Battle Ahead

God's greatest communications can only be made by His servants whose own hearts have been broken. The instrument in God's hands must personally be ready to share in suffering with others, just as Jesus's body was broken for us.
—Dr. Henrietta C. Mears, *What the Bible Is All About*

You can't do this alone. If you haven't fully accepted that, ask God for wisdom to understand as you read this chapter. Chances are, the Enemy has already tricked you into thinking you are alone, which is why you are reading this. He wants you in that mindset because he knows if you feel desperately alone, you will likely fail. Celibacy is not something you can do alone.

It sounds rather ironic since the entire notion of celibacy seems to be one of loneliness and longing. I'm here to tell you that if you believe this, you've been deceived. Now that's not to say there aren't great challenges with celibacy and abstinence. That's actually the whole purpose of this chapter, because there often isn't enough real talk about this in the church. So first, let's understand exactly what being celibate actually means.

You've likely heard a few different words used interchangeably when it comes to the practice of refraining from sexual relationships and pursuing sexual purity. Celibacy, abstinence, and fasting are three common ones. Here's the difference:

- Celibacy is abstaining from marriage and sexual relations.
- Abstinence is restraining oneself from indulging in something and is often used in reference to alcohol.
- Fasting is abstaining from a particular item or practice for a period and usually stems from a spiritual or religious calling to do so.

There are obviously similarities between the terms, and in some cases, people use them interchangeably. In other places in this book I've referenced abstinence specifically pertaining to refraining from sexuality during a period of singleness. But I've chosen to use the term celibacy here in this chapter because if you are single (not married) and not engaging with anyone sexually, then for the time being you are celibate. That doesn't mean you have professed a celibate lifestyle forever. It means that's what you're dealing with for this current season. Celibacy, as it is defined here, is God's design for singleness. God wants us to embrace our current status as an act of trust in Him rather than focusing on what we think we lack.

In whatever season we are in, we can incorrectly assume that those in different seasons aren't facing challenges like we are. We may think that the grass is greener on the other side, but that's not accurate. Being single is a trial. Being married is a trial. The Bible reveals that the entire Christian walk is a trial. So as a Christian, if you focus on what you think you lack instead of resting in God's sovereign plan for your good, you'll always consider the grass to be greener somewhere else. If you're not a Christian, you will believe the same thing but without the hope of reassurance of the Savior's plan for your well-being.

Even though I'm now a happily married woman on the other side, I haven't forgotten the intense difficulty of celibacy or singleness. I haven't forgotten where I've come from. The passion in me still burns in a way that no one except Jesus will ever quench. It's still there. It's just different now. Passion isn't quenched by marriage alone. Finding greener grass isn't the solution. Finding and abiding in Jesus is.

Within the Silence of Celibacy

First, the reality is that celibacy is usually not a frequent topic of conversation in church, among friends, or in the media. Like most things, there's good and bad to that. The good news is that there isn't an avalanche of advice on helping people not to have sex. That would be much like sitting in front of chocolate cake while you're on a diet. It would only increase temptation, not quell it. The other good news is that you'll less likely be led astray by false information on the topic.

The bad news is that most people don't know where to go to talk about celibacy, and most don't know how to counsel someone going through it, especially if they haven't successfully endured the struggle themselves. The Bible is sufficient in instructing us how to deal with any problem in life, but it does add a great deal to the conversation when the person giving advice has successfully overcome the issue at hand. I'm grateful you're reading this, but if you're going to talk to someone, I encourage you to seek those who have specifically had success in this area.

The other bad news about celibacy not being discussed openly is that because it is not a popular notion these days, there is a risk that those who bring it up will be pressured to conform to the rest of the world, which scoffs at celibacy. This makes it sounds increasingly lonely then, right? Keep reading.

Setting Your Sight

If you are single and you proceed in obedience by making the commitment to be celibate, you are going to experience a God-led, empowering journey outside of the realm of all popular culture. The only way to reach that destination is with the Holy Spirit leading you in the same way He led Jesus. Remember when the angels attended to Jesus (Matt. 4:11) after He was led into the wilderness? The only way there and back is with the strength and guidance of the Holy Spirit. The Holy Spirit is real. He's not some made up floating-on-clouds mystical entity. If you've accepted Jesus as your Savior, the Holy Spirit is about to lead you through a journey that will create a superwoman out of you. While the world looks down on the notion of celibacy, the strength and self-discipline of a faithful, Holy Spirit-controlled Christian single might be compared to the level of commitment required of a Navy SEAL, especially for a passionate person. You are about to be made truly distinguished, set aside for God's purpose, and if it's in His plan, prepared eventually for the best sex possible.

That right there was my driving force throughout my journey. I love sex. Not ashamed to say it. I absolutely love sex. Quite honestly, I was tired of settling. I wanted only the very best. And my thought was that the way to the best sex possible could only be by the One who created it. The fact is that my God doesn't want me to settle either. He also wants the very best for me, which is why He would even consider giving me Jesus. So I knew that if both God and I were aligned on me only having the best, He would also empower me to get there.

I am no less of a sinner than Saul (before he became the apostle Paul), who was so hostile to the true things of God that he killed people who professed Christ as Savior. I used to make fun of people like me who would say crazy things like "Jesus empowers me to have great sex." I absolutely would still be the same person making fun of people like me had He not proved to me that He does empower me to do all things that are aligned with His will. And yes, most especially, great sex within marriage.

I am living proof that celibacy during the appropriate season is absolutely the God-blessed, God-led, Holy Spirit-empowered road to the best sex you've ever had. Cheers and amen to that.

THE UNANTICIPATED SIDE EFFECTS OF CELIBACY

Now let's talk about the side effects of the journey. They were unanticipated for me, and that created more of a struggle at the time because I didn't know if they were normal or not. My hope is that they won't be unanticipated for you if you take this information into account. I want you to be well prepared.

YOU WILL BE LIED TO EVERY DAY

The Enemy will try to convince you every single day that you're missing out and setting yourself up for failure. He'll plant this idea in your mind and will use others to ensure that you hear it audibly as well. He will tell you that if someone loves you, it's okay to have sex before marriage; God understands, He made you that way. He will tell you that it's especially okay once you're engaged because you've already made the commitment in your hearts.

He'll tell you that it's entirely unrealistic to expect a potential spouse, especially a man, to be willing to see this commitment through, and that you'll just be pushing a good man away if you insist on him remaining celibate with you to the altar. He will tell you that God forgives and will bless your marriage and your union anyway. He will even tell you that you will learn a great deal, even necessary information, about the person you are with just by engaging sexually. He will tell you that it's just plain ignorant to even consider marrying someone whom you don't know if you are sexually compatible with. Or one of the more absurd ones, that if you don't feed your sex drive, it will shrivel up and die. You need to keep it in good working order if you ever expect to enjoy it later.

I've heard every one of these attempted justifications. And while some are half-truths (God forgives, He made you this way, and He understands the struggle with the temptation), these half-truths are all lies because they're used against the things that God wants for you. You can see how Scripture confirms every one of these as a lie in the next chapter.

Think about it. If God has planned the ministry of marriage in your future and if Satan is actively attacking you in the area of purity, isn't this even more proof that God has planned an incredible gift for you? The Enemy will go to great trouble to try to prevent a blessing that God has already prepared for you. Satan will consistently attack you to make you think you've missed the mark, when in reality God has already prepared a trophy for your victory. The Enemy has enough insight to see into your future. The question is, do you?

YOU WILL BE TEMPTED

Is this an unanticipated side effect? In a sense, no. Of course you're going to be tempted to have sex. But in another sense, yes. Get ready to be tempted by things that never had a pull on you before. Many people exchange one addiction or lust for another. During my journey of celibacy, I noticed I started to drink wine more. I never got addicted, but it certainly could have gone that way if I hadn't noticed a pattern of going to it every time I was particularly struggling. Sure, sexual temptations are going to come your way—especially when you aren't even expecting them—through images in media, words in songs, movie scenes, overheard conversations, and more.

But temptation will come from another direction too. If you're successful in fleeing from sexual temptation, the Enemy will still remain prowling in careful watch (1 Peter 5:8), seeking to understand where you may have another weakness. To understand what that is and to be prepared, consider the things that bring you the most comfort when you're in a place of struggle. Where are your outlets for your passion? What do you not abstain from that you feel passionate about? Even if they're healthy, godly outlets, be prepared to cover those areas in prayer and, if possible, godly accountability with a trusted friend.

YOUR APPETITES WILL CHANGE

Your appetites go hand in hand with the temptation. When someone loses one of their senses, often other senses seem to heighten to compensate for a lack of the missing sense's experience. Our bodies are in constant adjustment in relation to what is being experienced or shifted at any given time. When a woman is pregnant, she'll often develop a craving or distaste for certain foods or smells. Consider this time as one in which you're pregnant with the next season of your life. When our bodies go through a shift, it's felt in areas and systems other than just the obvious one.

For example, certain foods became almost euphoric and sensual to me during my period of celibacy. The touch of a hand or a hug from a friend became even more comforting than I had ever felt them before. A good laugh provided more of a release than it had previously. And a good workout was incredibly satisfying, especially when I drained myself of energy.

Even my view of certain things in nature became heightened, as though I had somehow been clouded from seeing how beautiful they were. There was a radiance I had never seen before in ordinary things around me. These moments of enjoying life in new ways were unexpected blessings from God that provided beauty in the season. Again, just be cautious to never enjoy any of that without enjoying God more. Enjoy the creation, and the Creator even more so.

Your Weight May Change— Not Necessarily for the Worse

Sex burns calories. If you were used to having sex regularly and are not now, that change may impact your caloric burn and thus your weight. While it may not be a drastic change in caloric burn, especially if you are not a sedentary person to begin with, it's another aspect of your fitness routine that you may want to consider compensating for with some additional exercise. Additionally, stress changes how your body carries weight. Depending on how you specifically deal with stress and adjustment, your appetite may increase or decrease. You may want to go to food for comfort, or you may want to exercise more to deal with the energy that you may feel in abundance at times.

I ended up losing weight during this time, partly because I wanted to keep myself looking good for when I would start to date, and also because I was getting a good amount of exercise to manage my energy. Another factor in my weight loss was that I would try to sleep more. Nights for me were heightened when it came to food and sexual temptation, so if I could get to sleep earlier, I could make it through the night. With proper sleep your body works better and burns calories more efficiently, and you can't eat while you sleep, so that's a plus. And it goes without saying that we are better able to handle stress with healthy sleep habits as well.

Weight change isn't necessarily bad news. All this is normal. When the scale changes one way or another, don't freak out. Know it is all part of the process, and consider what needs to be balanced out to stay at a healthy weight.

THE NEED FOR HEIGHTENED SECURITY

You will need to accept the fact that you have just been placed on duty day and night to be your own bouncer. You will encounter people who shouldn't be near you, images that shouldn't be near you, and thoughts that shouldn't be near you—to the degree that they will seem like magnets pulling you in. Ex-boyfriends will come out of the woodwork. Memories that you had long forgotten about will surface. People will invite you places where you shouldn't be. This is all part of the attack and lies of the Enemy, but you should be prepared that you—empowered by the Holy Spirit—are the only one who can physically separate yourself from temptation.

A bouncer physically throws unwanted visitors out. Your job also will literally be physical. Be prepared to get up, leave the room, leave the party, turn your eyes away, change the station, hang up the phone, block the text, and quickly get to God—especially when you feel tired. Don't underestimate the importance of staying on your post in this duty. Remember that you are being prepared for something amazing. Do your job well now so you will fully understand the benefits of it later. Who do you think experiences the most satisfaction getting to the top of a mountain: the one who took the lift up or the one who climbed it?

WEEPING AND GNASHING OF TEETH

Some of my dark moments were so difficult. My prayer is that you do not face struggles and difficult times, but I also know that a Christian truly seeking the Lord is bound to do so as part of an ongoing consecration process. As a very passionate woman, I can tell you that I endured nights of practically screaming into my pillow, even shaking from the overwhelming desire just to be touched. Those moments made it feel like there was no way out except to have sex. But that was a lie. Every single one of these dark moments was temporary. The Bible reminds us that "Weeping may endure for a night, but joy comes in the morning" (Ps. 30:5 NKJV).

You would be wise to anticipate the storms that will come and to prepare for them ahead of time. Most importantly, don't blow up your phone trying to find solace in someone else. Even if you aren't having sex the next day, I guarantee that the emotional anguish of this period will pass. Be prepared for it to come and go from time to time. But know that it will go more quickly and with less harm to you through the power of prayer.

Remember that you are being set aside for a great purpose. It's nearly impossible not to feel some pain in this period of growth. Also remember that if God is preparing a spouse for you, that man is enduring the same struggle. You want him to succeed for your future together. Take your mind off the present struggle, focus on God, and use that energy in the best possible way. Pray for your future husband's endurance. Imagine how loved he will feel when he finds out *you* were praying him through.

While it may sound completely contradictory to what you want to do, serving someone else in your greatest hour of need is the quickest way to restore your hope, positive energy, and ability to patiently endure. You don't have to believe me. Just try it. (Check out more on this in the chapter "Put On, Put Off.")

DEALING WITH THE PERCEPTION OF LONELINESS

I said at the beginning of this chapter that you can't do this alone, but perhaps that message seems unclear because the principle of being set aside naturally suggests separation. Your perception of your environment or current status is a foundational element of your success or struggle. If you're resting on God's promises and confirmation of your identity in Him, then you'll be significantly more prepared to handle the challenges than if you focus on who or what else you see around you.

Consider this analogy. Many brides choose to get dressed for their wedding by themselves or at least to have moments by themselves in preparation for the ceremony. Many fighters take moments on their own before going out into the ring. Warriors often prepare for battle with moments of quiet solitude. There are incredible biblical accounts of Jesus going away to pray by Himself, David crying out in solitude to God, and even Paul walking alone between evangelical outreach missions. Did this mean any of them were lonely? No. They were in intense preparation. How you view your current situation makes a great difference.

ACCOUNTABILITY WITH A FEW TRUSTED ADVISERS

Pray for the Lord to provide godly accountability. Don't automatically go to your best friend unless she is fully capable and interested in supporting you in the journey of celibacy. And you need to make sure your friend is a believer. Remember, you're in the Navy SEALs of Christian singleness. You need a strong believer versed in the Word who will be able to speak God's love and life over you in times of need. You need someone trustworthy who is completely convinced that this is a worthwhile investment for you.

If you're uncertain of who this is in your life, pray and ask God to lead you to one or more accountability partners. You do not need a plethora of people. Having too many could work against you. You do not need to join a support group. In fact, I would strongly suggest you don't. A bunch of people sitting around talking about their struggle of not having sex can be a constant, dangerous reminder to you of how "heavy" the burden is. Remember that Jesus said that He will take the burden and give you a lighter one (Matt. 11:28–30). He didn't say to get a support group. I'm not saying there isn't value in support groups for various reasons, but for this issue I would advise against it. Fellowship is important, but you need a few trusted confidants here, not a multitude of people you may have to guard yourself against. You will have enough to guard against without adding more.

A great accountability partner during a time of celibacy will remind you of the value of this calling, your worth in Christ, and the invaluable pursuit of holiness in a world gone wild.

NONSEXUAL BONDING WITH YOUR PARTNER

Next, if God crosses your path with the spouse He has chosen for you, this person will join with you to honor the commitment. This is where you will see the true bonding that occurs in the fire of trials. Fellowship will take on a whole new level.

When we are weak, Holy Spirit power is magnified (2 Cor. 12:9). The Bible says that two believers are better than one—and if one falls, the other can help them up (Eccl. 4:10). God seeks to empower both you and your husband-to-be toward victory. Imagine witnessing the Holy Spirit working in your guy when you are weak. These are the kind of moments that will deepen your bond prior to marriage. For me, they provided ongoing reassurance that God was with us. While these moments are precious and so valuable, that shouldn't inspire you to purposely test your husband-to-be though. If you are both truly seeking God, your guy, like you, will be empowered even in your weakest times. The "burden" will no longer be yours alone—and that alone is cause for celebration.

If you have not yet met the person who will become your spouse, but you believe God has confirmed that marriage is the path for you, then be encouraged that this is your preparation period. (You'll read more on this in the section entitled "The Call to Marriage" within the chapter "The Boundaries of Burn.") What you are going through in this moment is being used to prepare you for your spouse, and ultimately for you to grow deeper in your relationship with your Creator. If you have not received confirmation from God as to whether marriage is in His plans for you, you can rest assured that this trial remains worthwhile. You are being prepared for the only perfect spouse there is. As a believer, regardless of your marital status on earth, you are the bride of Christ. And as such, there is no greater call than to that of holy living for Him.

THE HOLY SPIRIT INSIDE YOU

While we touched on it briefly already, the power of the Holy Spirit is typically underappreciated. Yet it is this power that is the key to victory in the pursuit of purity. The gift of the Holy Spirit was meant to be your greatest and most personalized weapon in the battle ahead.

Before Jesus ascended, He assured His closest friends that they would not be alone and that He would send them a Comforter (John 14:26). He was referring to the Holy Spirit. If you're a believer, the Holy Spirit is literally dwelling within you. You can't get any more intimate than that. Think of the love that God has for us, that even in our humanity, He would choose to live inside us. He abides in us, as we abide in Him (John 15:4). There truly is no greater love.

Many people don't understand the power accessible to us because of His indwelling. You can't physically see the Holy Spirit, but you can ask Him to reveal Himself to you through His work. Be specific and truly genuine in your prayer if this is the desire of your heart. Then be prepared. If you seek Him with your whole heart, you will find Him (Jer. 29:13). In fact, your heart may be most primed to encounter Him in your darkest moments. That is reason alone to not be afraid of the night. He will be there and will possibly be even more palpable to you than before. He will be your Comforter.

Scripture says that we can be content with what we have because He will never leave nor forsake us (Heb. 13:5). Now is the time for you to embrace this truth and let it consume your thoughts, your will, and your emotions. There were nights when I asked God to let me feel His arms around me, as I longed for human companionship to do so. At the risk of sounding crazy, I can say with certainty that there were nights when I felt Him physically near me. I wanted human physical touch, but what I felt from Him was not that. It was something different, and it was more comforting. The Word says we can ask, and if we believe and it is aligned with His will, we will receive (Matt. 7:7; 21:22). Do your part to do the asking and the believing, and then proceed in trust.

Please remember that I never thought I'd be writing these words. The presence of the Lord your God is the greatest, most fully satisfying thing you can experience. I know because it has happened to me. And you can experience that right now. It's yours for the taking. You need not wait on anyone or anything else for that to happen. The comfort of all-consuming, unconditional love is available to you in the present moment. He's yours now.

The way to manage celibacy, like anything else in life, is with Him. You can step out onto the battlefield and know for sure that you are not alone. You are equipped and you are being prepared to fight the good fight, keep the faith, and finish well (2 Tim. 4:7). You can do this because He's with you and for you.

> And be sure of this: I am with you always, even to
> the end of the age.
> (Matt. 28:20 NLT)

CHAPTER 4

The Enemy's Plan against Purity: A View from Earth and Hell

Let us draw near to God with a sincere heart and with the full assurance that faith brings, having our hearts sprinkled to cleanse us from a guilty conscience and having our bodies washed with pure water.
(Heb. 10:22)

It was girls' night out, and we started the night off at my friend's house. All of us were single (newly single in my case) and were able to relate to one another and share some hilarious dating stories. As we sat on the couch, I boldly explained (even though I couldn't believe I was saying it out loud) that I had decided I wasn't going to date a guy unless he committed to refraining from sex until marriage. Knowing I had claimed to be recently saved and committed to living differently, my friends conjured up a couple patronizing smiles and nods joined with statements such as, "That's good if that works for you." One of them went further to tell me that I was completely unrealistic and that there was no chance of me finding a man (especially at this stage in life) who would agree to that. She suggested that I lower my expectations if I ever hoped to get married again. I'm grateful to know that even in my hurt, I knew this was a lie, and I rebuked it. I told her that if she ever saw me walk down the aisle again she would know that specific criteria had been met, because I wouldn't walk down the aisle otherwise. She was at my wedding less than eighteen months later.

There were several problems with this situation. First and most obviously was the crowd I was hanging out with. Sister, if you decide to commit to sexual purity, you definitely need to surround yourself with other sisters who are going to applaud and not criticize such a choice. Don't get me wrong—I didn't then, or now, consider these specific friends as enemies, but I now see how the actual enemy—Satan—was indeed using them. You will need sisters who are well versed in the Word to be able to help you recognize the tactics of the true enemy. These are the women who will reassure you and stand guard with you when the going gets tough.

Second, I realized that many others would also face opposing voices like I did in making a choice for purity. I believed my group was an accurate representation of the worldly view that tells us that we are risking a great deal by pursuing sexual purity and God's ways. I began to understand that other sisters out there were actively facing this challenge as well. It moved me to want to tell others how I debunked the lies that came at me hard and fast (even from friends) in the hopes that those others would armor up and deflect them faster than I did.

THE VOICE OF THE ENEMY

I want to use my experience to help you prepare ahead of time, my sister, to hear all the lies—"the risks" the Enemy will throw out at you from all angles and from people you may not be expecting to be used for his purposes. The following are actual statements that I heard, personally thought, or have heard other people claim against sexual purity. Following each lie below is the truth as applied from God's Word.

It's unrealistic to expect that in our current culture you're going to find a man willing to commit to sexual purity before marriage. And if you do, he'll probably be some asexual nerd who probably has never had sex anyway.

The Bible says, "With God all things are possible" (Matt. 19:26), and that He can empower us to do all things that align with His will through the power of Christ (Phil. 4:13). So if you're a Christian woman seeking a Christian man, God has this covered, and He may be preparing you to be a testimony to His power, just as He used me in this way.

Our society's negative view of abstinence overemphasizes worldly concerns and completely ignores the overarching benefits and wisdom of sexual purity. The most helpful thing I did in dating was to purposely seek out a guy willing to commit to sexual purity prior to marriage. It weeded out many men who would have led me in harmful ways. Conversely, the ones who stuck around after that conversation began to grow in their own attractiveness because of their holy and noble pursuit. In other words, their genuine reaction to this conversation showed me a whole different side of them that I wouldn't have been able to see otherwise.

It's similar to how many women (myself included) are attracted to men in uniform. Sister, a man in holy uniform (in training and pursuit of Jesus) is wearing the most attractive appearance-enhancer there is. I humbly confirm that during dating I met a few very attractive Christian men who were willing to commit in this way—and I married the hottest one I found. (And because God knows me so well, He actually gave me a man in uniform. Navy! Hallelujah!)

Yes, it's rare to find an adult man in our hypersexualized society who is still a virgin before marriage, but unlike what the world says, it's precious in God's sight. And if he's your husband, what a precious gift indeed. While a man living up to this calling may not be shouting from the rooftops how excited he is to be in a season of celibacy, that doesn't mean he doesn't exist. And that kind of man will genuinely be excited to meet a woman willing to come alongside him in that humble and difficult calling and see him through to the end of it.

It's completely realistic to find what God wants for you. While none of us know His timing, we do know it's always perfect and that it doesn't have to take long at all. Our God created the entire world in six days. Don't you think He can handle one strong man for you? You may be looking for one in a million, but God brought me my one in seven billion and ushered him into my life almost immediately after that conversation with my girlfriends that I referred to earlier. If you're aligned with His will and seeking Him fully, it's inevitable that you'll be surrounded with the manifestation of His promises to you the very moment the time is right. And His timing, in whatever His good plan is for you, is absolutely worth the wait. In fact, it's magnificent. Won't it be fun to see who is watching when the radiance of it all surrounds you?

It's unrealistic to expect two sexually interested adults to wait until marriage.

Why? If you became allergic to chocolate today and your doctor told you that you needed to refrain from it for the rest of your life to avoid a life-threatening situation, would you still take the risk of eating chocolate? I'm not saying you wouldn't be tempted—of course you would, especially if you love chocolate the way I do. But it's as simple as just choosing not to eat it. The chocolate doesn't have control over you. It has no ability in itself to make you do something you simply choose not to do. The same is true of our sexual desire. And yes, there are indeed life-threatening risks in unholy sexual activity.

Here's another perspective. Have you ever told your girlfriends that you've decided to lose weight or train for a marathon? What do you get most of the time? Applause and a bunch of cheerleaders! Most people applaud goals like that because our society holds them up as worthwhile achievements that don't offend anyone. Everyone sees the health benefits involved in goals such as weight loss, marathons, or other endurance events. Although most people also recognize the extreme requirement for self-control and discipline during those pursuits, there's no shortage of people pursuing those goals and encouraging you to do the same. There are retail stores, TV shows, classes, books, blogs, websites, and apps devoted to a healthier you, to weight-loss techniques, and to athletes committed to extreme goals.

There's actually a much greater risk of injury while participating in an extreme athletic event than there will ever be in pursuing sexual purity. So with this in mind, it's not true that it's unrealistic for two adults to wait until marriage to have sex. People often refrain from all sorts of things for religious, personal, environmental, or health reasons for much longer and in more extreme ways than sexual purity requires. Many commit to organic, vegan, or "clean" food lifestyles without multitudes of critics claiming that it is unrealistic, unwise, or harmful. And for some people like myself, committing to a vegan lifestyle would actually feel like an extreme goal!

So why are there such intense attacks on celibacy? It's because sexual purity offends Satan and overcomes his plans to destroy you. He will turn the whole world against you to convince you that you can't handle the self-restraint of celibacy. Satan knows that if you ever discover the low cost and great benefits of sexual purity, you'll realize that you have nothing to lose and everything to gain.

The goal of pursuing sexual purity before marriage doesn't even have to be extreme by worldly standards. Some athletes train for years in preparation for a short competition. Just ask Olympic hopefuls. They'll spend years in intense training for an event that lasts just seconds or minutes.

If you're dating a God-fearing Christian man, you may not even date as long as an athlete trains for an event. Who says you'll need to wait years before marriage? When God clearly shows His direction for you both to proceed to marriage, then you proceed. In my case it was only about fourteen months after Geoff and I started dating that we married. And the event you're training for—God willing—will last significantly longer than a few minutes. This is not a one-and-done kind of event with the momentary high of a trophy that you may or may not ever earn again. With God's blessing it will be a lifetime of enjoyment. Can someone give me a hallelujah?

So let's put this in realistic terms. Pursuing sexual purity is a commitment for a healthier, more discerning you, a better relationship with God, and a deeper connection with your future spouse. These results provide benefits that will pay off for the rest of your life and blessings that typically multiply over time. I'd take that any day over being the next extreme athletic champion.

You'll have no way of knowing if you're sexually compatible with your partner if you don't test it out before marriage. That's just going into things blindly.

Again, most people don't criticize vegans, for example, saying they're blind and ignorant for not eating a hamburger. I'm not personally a vegan, but I can certainly understand how someone could live a very healthy lifestyle as a vegan and not feel like they've missed out on anything. And I don't want to protest a lifestyle that requires such personal commitment. No one else is harmed by their choice. The same goes for a commitment to remain celibate before marriage.

It makes you wonder what could be at stake, then, for the person who is willing to criticize a choice for sexual purity as harshly as my friends did. The answer is that there is a great deal at stake for them. Those who are promiscuous are on the path to destruction, have given that which they can never get back, and may pay the price for a lifetime. Those who are sexually pure, however, have nothing to lose because they've given nothing away. There are only benefits to gain. So the reason why bystanders are offended by our commitment to sexual purity is that our choice reveals and highlights their loss.

The idea that you need to "test drive" your sexual compatibility before marriage is a lie from the devil that I cover later in the chapter "The Wise Listen to Counsel." If you're currently stuck in this deception, jump ahead and read that section and then return here.

So you expect me to be some pure, hand-holding, tight-lipped-kissing, turtleneck-wearing, chastity-promoting woman while I'm looking for a hot man who believes in great passion in a marriage like I do? How do these go together? Where's the romance in that?

This might be my favorite part to write because I actually used to criticize other people for the same thing, and I delight in how far God has brought me from that attitude. No, I don't exactly fit the description above, but, sister, I don't think you need to either in order to fully pursue God's path. The issue of our outward appearance (modest dress, etc.) is covered more in the chapter "Put on, Put Off," and it's important to learn how God expects us to care for the beauty He's created us with. But to diminish it to turtlenecks and tight lips is to miss so much of what He's capable of teaching you and wanting you to enjoy.

First, let's take this to the extreme. Do you realize that if God is truly capable of fulfilling all He promises in His Word, then you could have an arranged marriage—never meeting your husband until the moment of your vows—yet still have a God-blessed, passionate, committed, sexually compatible, romantic marriage? Our emphasis on what should go on in our courting, such as what he should look like and do, how we should dress and act, etc. doesn't matter nearly as much as we think it does, and certainly doesn't compare to God's sovereignty.

While we should keep our eyes open and understand how things may be impacted by our choices, God can make anything happen whether or not you are willing to align yourself with that plan. God can bring you a man who is incredibly conservative on the outside and amazingly dynamic in the bedroom, where only you get to enjoy it.

I want to debunk the overemphasis on romance as well—something I never, ever thought I would do. I'm not saying romance is bad. I have always loved it, and I still do. But I've learned that it's way overemphasized, especially in the dating and courting stages of relationships.

Sisters, is there truly any greater romance than an innocent man dying to save you? You're so precious in God's sight as His created and His beloved that He would have willingly been crucified just for you. You were worth the world to Him, and you still are. This isn't some cheesy motivational speech to make you feel better about yourself. This is truth that you need to adopt, claim, and remind yourself of daily. If you can understand the passion that Jesus Christ had for you that He would take unbearable pain and punishment so you wouldn't have to, you can understand that the romance box has already been checked once and for all. Pursued by the Creator of the entire world? There is no greater romance story. Ever. And it's yours.

That being said, romance that comes through your boyfriend or husband should be no more than icing on the cake. The cake should be God's love with the romance of Jesus Christ as the main ingredient, the primary flavor. Love and romance between husband and wife should be the savory icing. Icing is awesome, as we all know, but eating icing without cake is such a fleeting, diminishing, and ultimately disappointing experience. And sometimes the cake itself is so good that the icing is either unnecessary or even slightly distracting.

Let's talk woman to woman again. Ever have a guy tell you that you look beautiful while you're crying? (And I mean ugly crying.) For some of us, that could be the hook, line, and sinker to convince us that this man loves us for all eternity. It's certainly nice to hear that a man, especially a godly man, can find us beautiful even when we feel we're at our worst, but our barometers of love are so limited and temporary. Sisters, I speak to myself when I say that we can be so silly, so foolish with some of these ideas that we think measure success.

Since I got saved, my ideas of romance have changed so much. There was a time when I joked with a girlfriend that hearing "God music" during lovemaking would be an immediate mood killer. (How incredibly ignorant I was.) There was a time I would have never considered seriously dating a man who didn't at least occasionally bring me red roses and compliment my sexiness in some way. (Talk about worldly barometers.) And there was a time when if a man didn't make a big, *big* deal over Valentine's Day, I would have used that as a defining measure of his willingness to love and sacrifice for me. (I'm completely embarrassed to even write this now.)

Ladies, do you realize that Valentine's Day means nothing to Jesus? He didn't die on the cross holding a red rose for you because you were the hottest girl on the planet. He died on the cross draining out His red blood on the ground because you were a sinner in need of saving. He saw you as worthwhile from the inside out at your very worst and still chose to die for you. Hallmark can't produce on paper what Jesus produced for eternity.

Does God shun human romance? Of course not, and neither should you. Song of Solomon in the Old Testament is one of the most romantic books of all time because it's the foreplay dialogue of holy sexual union between two believers who have committed to each other in marriage. If God didn't consider romance good or intend it to be included in our marriage, He wouldn't have included it in the canon of Scripture. If you've never read Song of Solomon, take the time to read and reread it to hear what God wanted us to witness as holy human romance. Ladies, there are layers upon layers of meaning in what Solomon and his wife are saying to each other, and honestly, it's pretty hot!

Our worldly ideas of romance aren't accurate or trustworthy barometers for worthwhile, Christ-centered relationships. There's nothing more beautiful than a woman who combines the holy balance of confidence and humility to know and hold on to her worth as Christ's sacred bride. And the godly man whom God intends—and has specifically designed—to be your husband will be greatly moved by this image. If your own expectations of romance are in the way, you may miss the incredible romance God wants to reveal to you and how your husband's heart is deeply moved by God's presence through you.

I can tell you from personal experience of having men provide me the pinnacles of worldly romance that I previously used as barometers, not one of them compared to watching my husband try to maintain his composure as he gazed on me for the first time as his bride. And while I'm not saying this to boast in any way, I need to be clear that Geoff didn't skip romance in courting me.

The bottom line is that you're being deceived if you think you're risking or sacrificing romance to pursue God's path. God's path is beautiful, full of incredible surprises that have been custom designed with you in mind, all for His glory! He's created a plan to present your life as a beautifully pursued love story, ultimately between you and Him. If you finally take rest in this truth, you'll begin to see that His path is the one of ultimate romance.

It costs more money to do things to support sexual purity. If we go somewhere overnight, we would need separate hotel rooms. We would need separate houses to live in before marriage and gas in the car to go back and forth to visit regularly. Doesn't that seem financially irresponsible for two mature adults who can be saving money by at least paying rent together?

The logistics of financial choices and other living or travel arrangements are the temporary by-products of a choice that comes with lifelong benefits. Focusing solely on the short-term aspect of saving money isn't wise. If you're attempting sexual purity, you won't save enough money to compensate for placing yourself in unnecessarily tempting situations such as sharing a hotel room, apartment, or home. It's like sitting in front of a giant ice cream sundae while you're on a diet or going to a bar claiming that you'll "just have a soda" when you're trying to avoid alcohol. It's best to prepare a healthy and supportive environment so you can maintain your commitment and spare yourself a lot of unnecessary stress.

People generally don't criticize others who choose to make a financial investment to eat healthier. Remember, any such investment for sexual purity in the courting and dating stage is not meant to last permanently, because no one should have the goal of dating permanently. If we keep the bigger picture in mind, we're talking about a relatively short time considering the benefits to follow from such a wise choice. And sisters, joining finances before taking vows is one of the most foolish things you can do. It's a proclamation that the financial interest in the relationship is more important than the soul commitment.

It really comes down to deciding in your heart if a small financial expense to support your commitment is an investment or an inconvenience. An answer of it being an "inconvenience" reveals a divided heart, which leads to confusion and destruction. You'll need to decide whose plan is better, God's or yours. For a discussion of some of the aspects of godly conduct during dating—including living together—see the chapter "Real Submission."

God loves you and made you a sexual being with sexual needs. He certainly understands what you need, and even if you have a slipup once in a while, He will forgive you.

First, if this language doesn't immediately strike you as uncomfortably similar to the dialogue the serpent had with Eve in the Garden, then you probably haven't spent enough time studying that scene in Genesis. It's the first time a woman's emotions were manipulated to lead her into sin, and Satan has been recycling the strategy ever since. This rationale has his signature all over it.

Second, Jesus Himself warns us to be "as shrewd as snakes and as innocent as doves" (Matt. 10:16). So it's wise for us to recognize how the "snakes" formulate and package their lies. This statement above represents some of the standard packaging. If you break it down, you'll be able to more easily recognize it when it's spoken to you.

In order to gain your buy-in, the liar will typically phrase a lie sandwiched between two truths: God loves you and God forgives you. He did indeed make you exactly as you are, sexual desire and all. That's true. But in the middle, there's a twisting of the Word that implies that a little sin is okay because of those things, and therefore, we have some leeway to do what we want. Isn't that a message we'd all like to hear?

We tend to remember the beginning and the end of statements most clearly, so our recollection tells us that if those checked out as true, then what was in the middle is probably true too. False. The subtle twists don't usually catch our attention without Holy Spirit discernment. And these snakes in the grass are the most dangerous for us because we don't see them. This is why we need to listen carefully and to heed wise counsel, which provides accountability and support.

No one enjoys being in a relationship with a person who tries to get away with everything they can. And God doesn't desire that from you either. You're either with Him and pursuing His plan because you believe it's truly best, or you're following your own plan because you don't trust His. That doesn't mean you're perfect, but, sister, if you slip up, a heart that's bent toward God should follow suit in Holy Spirit discernment and conviction and proceed to repentance and confession and a request for forgiveness between you, God, and the one you slipped up with. True repentance means agreeing with God that what you did was wrong and turning away from it. Repentance means you don't repeat the behavior. A heart that dabbles in sin without acknowledging it as sin and repenting of it is a divided heart. God doesn't want part of your heart. He wants all of it. He's worthy of all the steps it takes to recognize and combat lies of the Enemy that keep your heart divided and out of sync with God's best.

Those who are leading you astray with statements like the one above simply don't know God's character. It's true that God loves you, forgives you, made you as you are, and knows all your needs. His love, forgiveness, and sovereignty over you, however, is not only undeserved but made more magnificent by the fact that He gives you free will to demonstrate your love for Him in return. It is our commitment to Him and the pursuit of holy living that reflects love for Him better than anything else we can do. Don't be deceived by the snakes in the grass.

If you're a virgin when you get married, you'll have nothing else to compare it to. You may not even know if you're having good sex.

The lies in this claim need to be exposed for what they are. First, we either believe that God's plan is best for us or we don't. Again, if you're not yet convinced, take a look at the chapter "The Wise Listen to Counsel" for a discussion of the "test drive" and all the implications that sexual experience has regarding what is meant to be sacred.

Second, it's another trick of the devil to tell you that he and God compare in any way. You can't compare Satan's way to God's way. You can't compare unholy sex to holy sex. You can't compare sin to blessing. There's no comparison, and there never has been. They're not in the same realm. Satan only has as much power as God allows and as you allow him to have over you. Satan's power is limited in reach, time, presence, and ability. God's power, on the other hand, is not limited by time, space, or anything or anyone. Satan's plans for you—including all the things that he wants you to believe you're missing out on—are indeed plans for you to miss out. He wants you to miss out on the blessing of believing and trusting God and ultimately experiencing what is truly the best. Satan wants to delay, destroy, and taint your experience as much as he can. He wants you to give it all away so your spouse misses out on your best as well.

Would you believe someone who said you could find the most precious, rare diamond in the world inside a plastic bubble in the gumball-vending machine at the supermarket? You wouldn't believe it because you'd clearly see from the cheap packaging that it couldn't possibly be the best. Comparison and competition are other cheap counterfeits that Satan offers. It's important to develop the ability to recognize and reject worthless substitutes for God's treasures. His best is the best. No one, no thing, and no experience can possibly compare.

If you are sexually frustrated, that can lead to other problems such as moodiness, distraction, and possibly even anger. You won't have a clear head because you'll be thinking about sex, and this may even skew your decision-making within dating.

When you hear someone claim this, ask them where that's found in the Bible. Of course, it's not in the Bible because it's not true. In fact, it's truly absurd. This type of thinking focuses entirely on a temporal, self-centered, and carnal view of sex. It goes against everything the Bible says about the benefits of holy living and the blessings associated with self-control and God-ordained sexual union. But let's examine this anyway because I want to share with you a great lesson I learned about sexual frustration.

Neither you nor your husband-to-be needs to live in sexual frustration. God did not intend for you to be sexually frustrated. I know that sounds contradictory if you're unmarried and are in touch with your sexual desires but are also trying to maintain holy celibacy. I want you to know that I learned this from a very personal place of being unnecessarily sexually frustrated for the first portion of the dating relationship with my husband, and then realizing later that it was unnecessary.

Sisters, again, some real talk. My body reacted the minute I met my husband. He was "it" for me. He checked all my boxes, and I truly believed he was the man God had sent, personally designed for me. I was attracted to him, heart, body, and soul. God's promise, I believed, had manifested before my eyes. What's not to get excited about?

Yet of course I wanted to maintain the call for both of us to refrain from sex before marriage. So I "managed" it on my own in other ways that provided a false and barely temporary sense of release. (Please see the answers I discovered about masturbation in the chapter "Put On, Put Off.") In hindsight, my understanding of how to "manage" my intense sexual desire for my husband-to-be through masturbation actually increased my frustration instead of diminishing it. My body wasn't craving me—it was craving him. Again, if we go back to the food analogies, which seem to work well, it's like having a specific, intense craving for cheese fries but constantly being given a baked potato. It may be a potato, but it's not addressing your craving for cheese fries. If anything, it's probably making you increasingly frustrated at the disappointing substitute. I can honestly tell you that for a long time I lived under the deception that masturbation was a viable solution. It wasn't.

But Satan wanted me there in a cloud of deception so he could potentially harm me and my husband-to-be. As I attempted to cool my flames on my own, I made the assumption that Geoff was also struggling immensely as well. That assumption introduced two very powerful yet subtle seeds that would form into weapons against our pursuit of purity.

First, the seed was planted that told me that Geoff was struggling and miserable also. If he was struggling and miserable, then wouldn't that mean he would look elsewhere for his happiness? How could I expect that he would maintain such misery for me? And wouldn't I be naïve to think he could? So maybe I should be proactive in helping to make sure that he was indeed not so frustrated. What if I skewed the boundaries a little bit just to help him out? Wow. Do you see the slippery slope my thought progression took? Do you see how fast that seed grew into an all-out weapon?

The truth? I finally approached Geoff to ask him about it. And ladies, I found the most surprising answer. My husband-to-be confirmed that he wasn't sexually frustrated. At all. He was "joyful." I kid you not. This is the word he used to describe what I was perceiving to be an incredibly difficult struggle that he was probably ready to give up on at any time. He instead said it was joyful because he knew what was waiting for him at the end. In fact, he reaffirmed that, even to his own surprise, this was the first time in his life that he wasn't at all sexually frustrated! This totally blew me away.

But, sigh. Satan didn't like that either. So he took it one step further to ensure that I would continue, at least temporarily, in deception and frustration. Ready for his next trick?

The next lie I heard was that Geoff's answer must have meant that he wasn't actually all that attracted to me. If he could control himself so well and I wasn't driving him mad with desire, especially at these beginning stages, then I probably wasn't such a turn-on to him after all. What would that look like years from now? Wasn't I the one he had dreamed of? If he had experienced all the excitement that I had in believing that God had made me exactly for him, then wouldn't he be reacting just as I was? So maybe that meant he didn't believe that like I did. What if I wasn't what I believed God had made me to be for Geoff?

I am astonished writing this years later, looking back, realizing the incredible, ridiculous, and all-out wicked train of thought that ran through my mind with Satan as the conductor during this time. Sister, these candid thoughts were nothing, nothing but wicked. They weren't from God. They were from the Enemy, who never wanted me to write the words you're about to read.

We overcame. Hallelujah! My husband-to-be took my hand and taught me—by walking it out in front of me—what choosing joy actually looked like. He was the first one to teach me how to actually be content in all circumstances and to see the joy of that which is yet to come and is promised by the Word of God. It was promised. It happened. I lived it. We overcame.

How is this possible? How can you do the same? By shifting your eyes and the determination of your heart toward truly pursuing purity empowered by the Holy Spirit.

Consider this. The fruit of the Spirit listed in Galatians 5:22–23 isn't conditional upon outward circumstances—married or unmarried, sexually active or sexually inactive, fed, hungry, clothed, naked, rich or poor. The fruit of the Spirit isn't based upon our feelings or perceptions. The fruit of the Spirit is alive and evident as the result of our simply living and abiding in Him no matter the circumstances.

Sisters, look, taste, and see how this fruit applies to our pursuit of sexual purity:

- Love—the exact thing you are craving from God and from your man.
- Joy—what we can choose instead of struggle and deception.
- Peace—the opposite of frustration. Jesus says He gives peace! (John 14:27)
- Patience—such a holy, beautiful statement of our love of God and one another.
- Kindness—definitely the opposite of unholy assumption or unnecessary self-affirmation.
- Goodness—the pursuit of a good thing together is even better than by yourself.
- Faithfulness—a beautiful, solid foundation for a relationship and a powerful statement about our faith in God.

- Gentleness—the opposite of aggression and self-seeking pleasure.
- Self-control—the ultimate characteristic of someone who, in pursuit of Jesus, is willing to die to their fleshly desires in order to place their love of you and Him first.

Can you honestly read this list and imagine a more attractive man than the one with these traits? Can you consider how beautiful a woman you are when you embrace the gifts of these as they are currently and readily available to you? This is the ultimate decision: to simply choose our own way or His. What's the destination worth to you?

Consider this analogy. We get in the car with a destination in mind. We turn the ignition and drive out on the road toward that destination, yet while we are behind the wheel, we take our eyes off the road and place them on ourselves. We have literally shifted our eyes from the road right in front of us (the one that will lead us to our destination) to ourselves in the mirror. Keeping our eyes there long enough will not only cause us to crash eventually, but will likely cause a crash so severe that we will never reach our destination at all.

We had done everything right by getting in the car, setting the correct destination on the GPS, and starting off toward it. Yet we missed the critical element of how to drive well, the choice to take the focus off ourselves and reach the desired worthwhile destination. It seems so simple to understand in driving, yet so complicated when it comes to everyday living.

There's no way to have a divided heart (or divided attention in this analogy) and arrive safely at His blessed destination. We can't keep one eye on the road and one eye somewhere else. God didn't design our vision like that, physically or spiritually.

One last thing. Sexual frustration, like any feeling or momentary experience, isn't limited to a marital status. If the goal of avoiding sexual frustration is the primary justification for having premarital sex, then it would also be a justification for having extramarital sex if the marital bed became a source of frustration. We can't invent a gray area of sin in one issue to justify our behavior and then claim it to be wrong in other ways that don't suit us.

This is the bottom line. Once I learned that the fruit of the Spirit was not conditional upon my desires being met or unmet in the current moment, I learned that sexual frustration had no power over me on its own and could indeed exist overshadowed by joy and peace. I'm not suggesting that contentment feels natural when you are denying the desires of your flesh. I wouldn't have honestly believed this to have been possible if I hadn't experienced it for myself. I'm confirming that it is entirely supernatural—and entirely possible (Phil. 4:13).

THE ENEMY MAY BE ALIVE, BUT HE IS ULTIMATELY DEFEATED

I wouldn't be surprised if you have heard at least most of these voices of the Enemy at some point or will hear them in the process of pursuing purity. Rest assured, though Satan is still alive and prowling around, he is ultimately defeated.

Jesus has overcome. And He's paved the way for you to do so with Him. There's no weapon formed against you or your holiness that can stand. He is faithful and He is true. But He wants you fully prepared for the journey, which takes us to our next stop on the tour of the grand distortion Satan is attempting in redefining natural sexuality.

CHAPTER 5

Exchanging the Natural: Homosexuality, Bisexuality, and "Try-Sexuality"

They exchanged the truth about God for a lie, and worshiped and served created things rather than the Creator—who is forever praised.
(Rom. 1:25)

There was nothing more natural than the first woman and man living in complete peace, nakedness, and transparency with their Creator. Satan had to pull a grand distortion in order to disrupt that. He relabeled what was directly in front of Eve by alluring her through her emotions. He convinced her that what was unnatural (breaking communion with God) was the better option. He appealed to her pride and hid and denied the truth of the death that would surely come through the deception. Satan convinced Eve to trust her emotions and appetite rather than God's instruction, resulting in her breaking communion with Him. This was the beginning of mankind exchanging good for evil and natural for unnatural.

We must understand that we don't have the right to rename what God has distinguished as natural and holy or unnatural and sinful.

In the dark time of my own distortion (at the beginning of this journey), I remember a day when I was sitting in a waiting room preparing for a session with my counselor. She had various decorations in the room, one of which was a sign that displayed someone saying, "If your love affair had to be secret, it wasn't good for you." I remember being angry about that sign, certain that no one could understand my circumstances, nor did anyone have the right to impose a judgment on my relationship. Ironically, in my sessions I had purposely not told my counselor about my current affair—with a woman. The Lord was trying to get my attention, but I was choosing to remain blind in my sin.

I believe now that it was quite literally a sign from God. While I didn't think it had any validity then, I understand it much differently now. Satan has made such a strong attack on sexuality—twisting sex to give it an unnatural allure like something illicit and hidden in the dark. He doesn't want us to see the light and beauty and holiness of God's plan for natural sex. Too many of us are allowing Satan to succeed in creating a norm out of what God refers to as unnatural, and we're getting desensitized so quickly to the power of this attack. For me, as soon as I stepped in it, I was able to justify that it, indeed, felt entirely natural. The allure was so strong it distorted my perception of it immediately.

I have learned from a very personal place that there is no good connotation around secretive or unnatural affairs, no matter how we try to justify them. But I also understand (again from a personal place) that there is certainly a fascination around it—one that Satan has had a great time using to seduce us, painting a picture of romance, excitement, and intensity in a way that we believe no one else but us (and our secretive lover) could understand. I justified the secrecy of my own affair in that same way, as something only the two of us would be able to fully comprehend. The isolation and taboo nature of the relationship made it even more enticing and exciting.

Satan has painted illicit affairs in colors that are bold and bright in an attempt to make marriage seem to be boring beige at best. No one refers to marriage as an affair. Most people have no idea how bold, bright, and hugely exciting marriage can be. And that deception is exactly where Satan wants us until we are convinced that the forbidden, that which is clearly illicit in God's eyes, is the better option, the only natural fit.

It was difficult to learn that I didn't have the right to rename or redefine what was right and wrong for myself. It took me realizing that Jesus is the source of truth (John 14:6) to understand that God's Word has already defined it clearly. There are multiple warnings and descriptions throughout Scripture of what God considers to be unnatural, especially in regard to sexual sin. In Romans 1:26, the Bible says that "God gave them over to their shameful lusts. Even their women exchanged natural sexual relations for unnatural ones." The NLT version specifies that the unnatural deeds included the women having sex with each other and the men having sex with each other as well (Rom. 1:26–27).

The Word of God refers to homosexual sin as unnatural and abominable (Rom. 1:26; Lev. 18:22; 20:13). The Bible is not unclear about this. There is no instance of homosexuality or unnatural sex in the Bible that isn't directly linked to sin. God's plan for sex is specifically between one man and one woman as husband and wife. Their bodies fit together perfectly. The bonding forms them into one flesh (Mark 10:8), and that one flesh is blessed as they are both in submission to the Holy Spirit. Anything outside of this natural sexual relationship of husband and wife is unnatural in God's eyes.

Because this book, and especially this section, focuses on sexual sin, I want to caution against trying to judge which sins are the worst. Not only does the Bible warn not to do that, but God doesn't see it that way either. Consider the following example. As much as I love the color red, if somewhere in the Bible, God said that the color red was sinful, I would do my best to avoid any trace of it in my life. If I lie, if I think an evil thought, if I murder someone, or if I have a sexual relationship with someone other than my spouse of the opposite sex, I am in sin.

This sounds extreme by worldly standards though. The world says we should be able to do whatever we want and that unnatural can be natural and wrong can be right. Yet there is still an obvious disconnect in the universal application of this thinking. For example, many groups exist to stop drunk driving. Why? Because we understand that certain behaviors are clearly dangerous to society and must be forbidden regardless of someone's feelings as to whether they think they should be able to drive or not. Many drunk drivers have gotten behind the wheel believing they were okay to drive. There is harm and consequence to sin regardless of what anyone thinks or feels about it ahead of time. And the choice to sin sexually with another is the choice to ensure that the responsibility and consequence of that sin not only falls on you but also on the one with whom you engage. There is no way to contain the danger of the unnatural.

In my sinful relationship there was nothing natural about what I was doing at the time. It didn't matter who I tried to hide it from or how I tried to justify it. And while the world today has largely accepted sex outside of the male-female marriage relationship, it doesn't mean that God has. That's the part that we as believers must stand firm in, declaring His Word to be the truth, even amid the shifting and distorted views of the world. The Word of God has not only confirmed what we can expect to see occur "unnaturally" but has some serious implications for rebellion as people continue to pursue and attempt to justify that which is clearly against God's plan.

THE LANDSCAPE OF REBELLION

The Bible says that because of our rebellion, we're getting closer and closer to His ultimate wrath, the final judgment. If you look at this description of the last days, it's hard to imagine that we aren't indeed part of it right now. It is most certainly applicable. Consider what Paul says to his beloved "son" Timothy:

> You should know this, Timothy, that in the last days there will be very difficult times. For people will love only themselves and their money. They will

be boastful and proud, scoffing at God, disobedient to their parents, and ungrateful. They will consider nothing sacred. They will be unloving and unforgiving; they will slander others and have no self-control. They will be cruel and hate what is good. They will betray their friends, be reckless, be puffed up with pride, and love pleasure rather than God. They will act religious, but they will reject the power that could make them godly. Stay away from people like that! They are the kind who work their way into people's homes and win the confidence of vulnerable women who are burdened with the guilt of sin and controlled by various desires.
(2 Tim. 3:1–6 NLT)

Sisters, if you are a passionate woman like me, I'm hoping you caught the warning here. Did you see how Paul refers to vulnerable women who are burdened with sin and controlled by "various desires?" You may not consider yourself vulnerable. I certainly didn't. But this was the exact deception that was used against me because of the intensity of my desires. I felt strong and established in my homemade boundaries of what was "natural" and good for me as I allowed the distortion to take root. Like the women Paul references, I had the same target on my back for Satan to take aim at, just as he did with the first woman.

From the first moment in the Garden, Satan began to distort the idea of what was good and natural by manipulating Eve's feelings. It is subtle and at first maybe even easy to miss, but look at the two translations below that reveal the steps in her deception:

> The woman was convinced. She saw that the tree was beautiful and its fruit looked delicious, and she wanted the wisdom it would give her. So she took some of the fruit and ate it.
> (Gen. 3:6 NLT)

> When the woman saw that the fruit of the tree was good for food and pleasing to the eye, and also desirable for gaining wisdom, she took some and ate it. She also gave some to her husband, who was with her, and he ate it.
> (Gen. 3:6)

What God told Eve was forbidden and wrong (and would even result in death) became "good" and nourishing, beautiful in appearance, and valuable for offering something she didn't have before. Satan took her previous natural understanding of God's instructions and twisted them to something unnatural. And then he twisted the unnatural to beautiful.

Of course, it didn't end there. The pattern of deception and distortion has multiplied and recycled in different ways throughout human existence. Today the world encourages people to indulge in "try-sexuality"—experimenting with any and all forms of sexuality that feel right. Almost every type of sexual deviation is considered good. There are currently so many initials and terms for sexual preferences, such as LGBTQ, pansexual (I had to look up that one), bisexual, asexual, and more being developed regularly. It seems as long as there's a new label and someone to join in and claim it, then it must be acceptable.

Do you see the parallel? Satan is systematically using our sin nature to make what's unnatural and harmful seem normal and good. And he's doing it on a grand scale—no longer one isolated deception at a time. The landscape is becoming more and more slippery and distorted as we try to make heads or tails of what's right or wrong in our own understanding. God didn't want that burden on us though. He defined the boundaries of morality for us so we wouldn't have to, especially in these volatile times.

BORN THAT WAY?

I believe that somewhere within us many still consider what is natural to be best. We hear regular accolades for the benefits of natural childbirth, natural food, and natural household items such as cleaning or beauty supplies. While the natural choice doesn't always end up determining our preferences (I'm sorry, but cheese puffs are still awesome in my book), somewhere within we seem to still want to perpetuate the value of the natural. The truth is that what God created in its natural state is His best for us.

Unfortunately, Satan has caught wind of this too, so he's convinced plenty of people that they can now attempt to justify sin because it is something they believe they were "naturally born with." There is a great misunderstanding about the difference between being born *with a sin nature* and being born *as a particular sin*. We cannot attempt to justify sin with the implication that God has created sin as a natural part of our being. When God created man, he said it was "good." God wasn't then referring to and has never referred to sin as good. Adam and Eve weren't born with a sin nature. But when it entered into their lives by their choice, it was passed along to every subsequent generation. God does not contradict Himself and has not done so within any part of His creation. If God was okay with our now inherent sin nature, then Jesus's sacrifice wouldn't have been necessary.

In our world today, though, many people debate the question of whether it is possible to be born gay. As a Christian, I have a problem with any label contradicting what God has confirmed His children to be, especially that of something God considers as sin. Whether you are a Christian or not, if you're reading this, God isn't done with you yet, and you, also, should avoid confirming any label over yourself that isn't of Him. For me as a believer there are only two things confirmed in me: I'm saved by grace alone, and I'm His. I'm graced with those claims because He has called me to them and I have chosen to heed the call. I'm a Christian. Any other label would suggest that it has dominion over me the way Christ has dominion over me. The Bible confirms that nothing can separate me from His love (Rom. 8:38–39), so why would I want to label myself as something that separates me from my Lord and places it above His dominion?

The issue with trying to determine if someone could be born gay or not is not an issue with the particular word *gay,* but with the unnatural implication of how true identification is formed. The question in itself falls short because it doesn't recognize God's sovereign plan and the importance of our lifelong consecration. My friend Gary Schneider, founder and CEO of *Every Orphan's Hope,* explains that this question, like others identifying children born as orphans, for instance, determines condition as proper indication of lifelong identity. And when we make the mistake of doing that, we give Satan way too much leeway to call us by our sin and convince us that this accusation wasn't washed clean by the blood of Jesus Christ.

Maybe you're asking yourself what parallel the term *orphan* would have to the term *gay*. Well, as Gary educated me, in some cultures the term *orphan* carries a lifelong implication of shame and disgrace—even when the one carrying the title is not living in poverty or need at all. The world of these cultures has redefined a term that Jesus, Himself used to describe others in a way that did not carry shame or disgrace. The world has distorted and attempted to redefine the nature of the term, just as many have distorted the terms of *homosexuality* and other sexual sin. So one's understanding of the question of whether or not someone could be born gay depends on what their reference is for truth.

If you agree with God's Word and consider homosexuality to be a sin, the quick answer is that you cannot be born *as a sin*. You were created in God's image, and He did not make a mistake with you. If you are not a Christian, but you still believe certain things may be sinful, you could consider this question in another way. If it were possible to be born gay, is it also then possible to be born a murderer? That question gets significantly more uncomfortable because it's very hard to imagine an infant born to be a murderer—and most people consider murder to be sinful. The way we answer these questions depends on what we believe to be truth and what we believe to be sin. God's Word qualifies sin clearly. As a believer, I do not believe that anyone is born gay, a murderer, an adulterer, or any other sinful condition. I believe we are born with an inherited sin nature and with the choice and empowerment of the Holy Spirit to live otherwise.

I'm not making light of this discussion, but it really is the same thing as saying that you could be born with the desire to eat junk food every day. Sin is sin and we all have a tendency toward it. We're all born with at least the occasional desire or urge to lie, steal, or in other ways violate the rights of others, but society rightly expects us to control those urges. And God Himself will empower you to do what in your flesh you cannot fathom doing—to deny the flesh. Each of us is a sinner in need of a Savior, regardless of our particular inclinations and weaknesses. But when we try to determine truth based on our individual inclinations, we run into the same free-for-all, anything-goes attitude that is described in the Scripture referenced earlier pertaining to the last days (2 Tim. 3:1–6).

While some might call me a hypocrite in this area, I can deny that in good conscience because I personally understand the pull toward sexual sin. When I was in it, I thought someone of the same sex could relate to me more, accommodate me more, and could be more compatible with me. Eventually it felt so natural that I was convinced that this was the way I was made to experience love and that perhaps I had been looking in the wrong place every time before that. I honestly questioned if God had indeed made me that way. I have since found by my own experience that my questioning was not founded in the truth of God's Word, but rather, on Satan's lies.

UNFILTERED TRUTH

Just because I'm not currently engaging in sexual sin doesn't mean I don't have to fight my sinful nature and die to self every day for all the other sins I'm tempted to commit. My temptations now may look different than they did ten years ago, but they are not necessarily easier. My battle against sin is no more or no less of a reality than anyone else's. We either will continue in the battle or give in and pay the price. If we go by our feelings and we blur moral standards and social norms, then eventually nothing will be off limits. Unfortunately, our world is going in that direction very quickly, filtering "truth" to fit our perceived needs and to avoid offending anyone.

I have heard even well-known "Christian" celebrities make a gray area of what God says is black and white because they don't want to hurt people they love who are gay. They claim that we are simply to love everyone and leave the judging to God. I want to make clear that a Christian reflecting the truth of God accurately does not make them the judge. It makes them His ambassador

(2 Cor. 5:20). The Bible says, "Better is open rebuke than hidden love. Wounds from a friend can be trusted, but an enemy multiplies kisses" (Prov. 27:5–6). When we are willing to extend false affection toward a fellow sinner instead of offering them the rebuke that reflects truth, are we positioning ourselves as a true friend or as an enemy?

If I have one chance to tell you the unfiltered truth, I'll take it. You're being deceived if you think a sexual relationship outside of marriage of male husband and female wife is okay. It's not. We're getting used to a new and sinful norm because we're being desensitized to what is wrong.

As a culture, we need to stop taking sin so lightly.

As a woman, you need to stop taking sin so lightly.

I realize that I will be called judgmental, narrow-minded, or bigoted for saying that it's wrong to engage in a sexual relationship with someone other than a spouse of the opposite sex. But despite that, I'm not afraid to say it. It's wrong. Not because it's wrong in my book, but because it's wrong in His. I didn't write the Bible; I just choose to live by it because I know who wrote it. There are some things that are black and white.

The truth is that God has created mankind in His image (Gen. 1:27), yet because of the fall, everyone since Adam and Eve (with the exception of Jesus Christ) has also been born as a sinner in need of redemption. In other words, we are born as God's children (indeed, in His image), and simultaneously at birth we enter into the lifelong process of fighting against the sin nature we inherited because of the fall. Every one of us needs to continually fight temptation to sin, regardless of the nature of that temptation—but God has equipped us to do so. This is the whole beautiful point of the saving grace of Jesus Christ. God will empower us to live as He commands through the power of the Holy Spirit once we trust Jesus as Lord. He tells us that it's a daily decision to die to self (Luke 9:23). I am living proof that it is possible to choose to put the Lord's commands ahead of your own desires and to deny yourself for the sake of pleasing God.

LOVE GREATER THAN OUR DESIRES

Another great and unnatural distortion is the half-truth in the claim that you "can't choose" whom you love. As humans we are born to love. That is how God created us to be and how He's commanded us to live. We're supposed to love one another. The problem is not love. The problem comes when we choose to express that love in action that God doesn't bless. The choice for sin is the choice to be separate from our Creator. And that goes for any sin. God is love (1 John 4:8); therefore, love in its purest form cannot be sin. And if God names something as sin, it cannot be pure love. Many, many murders have been committed in the name of love. Claiming love as a motive has never been a justification for sin.

When I first got saved, I was still in my sexual sin and did not necessarily plan to stop. I wanted to feel loved. Everyone wants to feel loved; it's the most natural desire of all. There's no logical reason that I, for instance, would want to take an opposing political or religious view against the very thing I previously associated with love. Even as I slowly started to grasp that I was in sin, I honestly think I planned to live in both worlds for a while. I didn't realize it wasn't going to work (Matt. 6:24). I didn't realize that soon I wasn't even going to want it to work.

My entire worldview changed by the power of the Holy Spirit when He came to live inside me. When that happened, I lost my ability to associate sin with love. I gained discernment and conviction as to what God really does consider sin. I didn't plan or choose that. I didn't expect to change so drastically. When God's love began to take over my heart, I began living beyond my own initial desires. I was beginning to recognize love that went beyond feelings, logic, and even sometimes my own understanding of what was right and good. I was learning that making decisions based on feelings might have previously been convenient, but when not based in truth and God's direction, had significant consequences.

Follow me through this illustration. I love my sons like crazy. I keep my commitments to them, and they know if I tell them I'm picking them up somewhere, they can count on me being there. But what if one day I decide that instead of picking them up at school, I go to Costco instead and look for them there? After all, Costco is more convenient and fits my schedule better that day, especially since I have items on my shopping list for there. When I arrive at Costco, however, I'm angry that they're not there. But why should I be upset? Costco wasn't the agreed upon meeting spot. My kids are at school. I made a decision based on my feelings, and I'm upset it didn't work out. If I want to pick up my sons, I have to drive to school to get them because, regardless of my feelings about their location, I won't be able to find them at Costco. When I finally get through my internal struggle and go back to school to get them, I have undoubtedly hit traffic and am an hour late. They're frustrated, and so am I. The whole thing could have been avoided; furthermore, I missed out on an hour of time with my sons that day. This sounds ridiculous, right?

Most parents I know wouldn't do this because it would be considered negligent toward their kids. Most parents understand that making decisions based upon feelings isn't good parenting or care over their precious children. So why do we justify important decisions about the giving of our bodies as though feelings would be a proper barometer to do so?

God's plan for sexual relationships also sounds ridiculous to some because it doesn't fit their feelings. His plan is for sex to take place within the confines of marriage between a male husband and a female wife. We can experiment with other options, but His blessing and reward of true sexual pleasure won't be available through our alternate paths. True fulfillment can't be found any other way. Until you experience this, you may not know it for a fact, but I do because I have experienced it. My hope is that even if you don't believe me, you will believe Him. You don't have to go the wrong path and suffer like I did to learn the truth. And you don't need to be deceived by the grand distortion that Satan is trying to accomplish in this world. You can be a wise woman who is not on the shifting sand of the world, but rather is grounded in the Word of God.

Assuming marriage is in God's plan for you, you can rest assured that He planned one of the most incredible gifts you can ever experience to be your wedding gift. Nobody gets wedding gifts if they don't have a wedding. You can't pretend to have a different birthday just to get presents sooner. (I guess you can, but you can expect to lose some friends when they realize you made it up.) You simply can't create your own moral compass and expect God to bless the path you take. The Israelites had the promised land waiting for them, but because they tried to do it their way instead of God's, it took them forty years to get to it. Do you seriously want to wait a lifetime for good sex? You may think you're better off having it your own way, but that's like a fake birthday party (and there's fallout afterward).

Sexual sin isn't God's plan for you. To fully grasp what is sin and what's not, you have to understand God's message in His Word. And to understand God's message, you must have the Holy Spirit living inside you to help you hear His truth properly, or it will sound like foolishness (1 Cor. 1:18). In order to have the Holy Spirit living inside you, you must accept Jesus Christ as your Lord and Savior and believe that He was raised from the dead after dying to pay for your sins. There is no other way. Once you have the Holy Spirit residing in you, you will be empowered to live above your feelings and sinful tendencies no matter what form they take. No matter what you feel, there's nothing in your life that He can't redeem, restore, and renew.

It is not my job to convince you that this is the only way to freedom and joy. You can go your own way if you choose. That's the beauty of the gift of free will. But don't be deceived into thinking it's natural and good just because you believe it to be. You, my sister, don't need to be like the women Paul described, "burdened with the guilt of sin and controlled by various desires"

(2 Tim. 3:6 NLT). If you are in Christ, you are a free woman—unchained by desire, no matter what those desires look like. I understand it can be overwhelming and consuming, but there's hope because sin isn't the path of God's best for you.

If you get lost, there is one source of truth, one path. And it's written by the One who created every atom and molecule in your body and therefore knows every desire, every struggle, and every question you'll ever have in this life. He knows what you need to hear to address them. He says it in John 14:6:

I am the way and the truth and the life.

CHAPTER 6 ⸻⸻⸻⸻⸻⸻⸻⸻⸻⸻

The Boundaries of Burn: Foundational Steps in Pursuit of Purity

But if they cannot control themselves, they should marry, for it is better to marry than to burn with passion.
(1 Cor. 7:9)

Establishing and rooting yourself in truth and appropriate boundary lines is absolutely foundational prior to taking relational steps with someone else toward sexual purity. For me, stepping back into the dating scene was both strange and exciting at the same time. I had plenty of dating experience prior to my salvation experience, but now dating with Jesus at the center of my life seemed like an entirely different endeavor. I knew Jesus loved me and created me as I was, even with all my passion and hunger for companionship and affection, but I really didn't know what His boundaries looked like, practically speaking. And if I'm totally honest, my hunger for affection was possibly even stronger than my desire for companionship. I longed to feel someone lovingly touch me again.

Yet as we've established, God's Word commands celibacy during singleness. Even as a newly saved woman, though, I couldn't reconcile how to balance the desire that continued to rise in the absence of affection. Celibacy was not something I intended to celebrate; I didn't even know how to endure it. I didn't ever plan to be celibate, but I found myself there and now just wanted to know how to deal with it and if it actually meant that I couldn't do what I wanted to do. I started asking some questions and searching God's Word for what my parameters were.

PURSUING THE BOUNDARIES OF BURN

The verse at the beginning of this chapter (1 Corinthians 7:9) was the verse that spoke to me most deeply, likely because of the word *passion*. Having lived my old life with passion as the foundation, burning with passion was a lifestyle. I personally knew all about the burn from my previous behavior. But what did that mean now if I wanted to live a godly lifestyle? I didn't plan on being a nun, after all! I loved my passion. Did God really want me to live without it? Did it really mean that I couldn't enjoy affection with someone unless they were my spouse? Was I going to be one of those people who didn't kiss their spouse until they were pronounced husband and wife at the altar? Not knocking that choice, but I just couldn't see myself there—at all. I needed more information. I confess that I was looking for a list of acceptable and unacceptable activities. I don't want to give you false hope, though; God wasn't interested in my desire for that list. But what I found and what I heard got me through.

Since there is no list in the Bible of acceptable affection-based activities that are God-ordained prior to marriage, I had to start with the basics and ask God to help me to understand and build from there. According to 1 Corinthians 7:9, in the premarital stages it seems that we must avoid the burn. Often we will see words interchanged depending on which translation of the Bible we use. The term *burn*, however, is used in most of the popular translations available, including the New International Version, New American Standard Bible, New Living Translation, New King James Version, and King James Version. One translation, the New Revised Standard Version, uses the word *aflame* instead of *burn*. For the purposes of my search, I continued to examine the meaning behind the word *burn* as used in Scripture.

I found one of the best explanations of the term *burn* to be by Frederic Louis Godet,[1] which he used specifically in reference to this verse, stating that to burn is "the fire of inward lusts in conflict with conscience." Another commentary explains *burn* as "the secret flame of lust, which lays waste the whole inner man. The dew of God's grace is needed to stifle the flame, which otherwise would thrust men at last into hell-fire."[2]

From these two references alone, it was clear that burn territory is where our conscience becomes impacted, involved, and (hopefully) conflicted. Burn is where feelings and flesh take over. Tragically, burn territory is capable of laying waste or destroying the whole man. Note that it's not just laying waste a relationship; it is referring to the whole person. Lastly, we can deduce that the only salve to cool the burn is the dew of God's grace. Only God, *not you*, will be enough to prevent you from destroying *your whole self.*

Burn is the place where one's own selfish desires come first and God comes second. The boundary of that place is different for each of us, and it may be different for every relationship and for every circumstance as

---

1. Frederic Louis Godet, *Commentary on First Corinthians.* (1889; repr., Grand Rapids: Kregel Publications, 1997), 331.

2. Robert Jamieson, A. R. Fausset, and David Brown, *Commentary Critical and Explanatory on the Whole Bible.* (Oak Harbor, WA: Logos Research Systems, Inc., 1997.)

well. The burn can start slow and subtle or be fast and furious. The burn is therefore not necessarily predictable. Ironically, today burn is where most of society says that it's okay to live, putting yourself first and doing what feels right. But burn is never okay with God because He loves you and wants you safe—not burning.

So how do we practically apply this to premarital relationships? In my journey, often through trial and error but with a willing heart, I found five critical steps that provided the foundation for the rest of the learning.

1. Communicate Up; Write it Down

If you're a believer, the first step is for you to directly ask God to define what burn looks like for you specifically. You need to be honest with yourself about what you hear from God and write it down. The Enemy will distort this for you later (in the heat of the moment as he did with Eve), so you need to have it written clearly somewhere for accountability. James 4:17 says, "If anyone, then, knows the good they ought to do and doesn't do it, it is sin for them." This is why personal accountability is critical.

Remember, though, that prayer should not be a one-way conversation. Upward communication also includes downward response. If you are not sure if what you have heard was the voice of God, check it against

Scripture. God's voice will never contradict Scripture, but Satan's always will.

2. COMMUNICATE LATERALLY

Following the first step, you need to talk with whomever you are in relationship with to ask what burn territory looks like for him. I once dated a man who responded that anything that got him turned on would be this forbidden territory. He was convinced that if we proceeded toward courtship and engagement, it wouldn't be safe for us to be in any circumstance where he got turned on with me. I confess truthfully that part of me was disappointed that if I stayed with this man I would know nothing of his passion for me prior to marriage. That sounded dull. And then another part of me thought (pridefully) that it must mean he has such an abundance of passion for me that he wouldn't be able to control himself—that I was just that hot. I literally am laughing out loud at myself and shaking my head, as I am mortified to acknowledge, let alone write these words. But for the purpose of this testimony, it is powerful to understand how much of a god passion was to me.

So what did I do with this? I didn't think God needed me confined to a relationship that was void of anything affectionate or exciting, but I knew He also had a boundary for me that I shouldn't cross. Where was that?

I asked around and found some godly people to get their advice, a different form of lateral communication that proved to be important in helping me navigate the noise in my head. Fellowship is important for many reasons, but in this case it helped me realize I wasn't alone in my quest for answers, which was reassuring and critical.

I heard advice that spanned the gamut. Some said that nothing of a sexual nature should go on between two Christians trying to remain pure before marriage. I heard people say that kissing and even holding hands could be dangerous, forbidden territory. (For some, it very well may be.) I heard others claim that as long as intercourse didn't happen, all else was allowed. Another point of view was that I was supposed to just handle my sexual needs "on my own." (See my exploration of the topic of masturbation in the chapter "Put On, Put Off.")

Now remember, any advice we get (even the best-intended advice) needs to be measured against God's Word. But since God's Word was not explicit about this topic, I continued to struggle greatly with this debate in my head. This takes us to our third step.

3. PRAY, WILLINGLY SEEK DISCERNMENT, CONFESS, REPENT, AND REPEAT

I did not want to dishonor God so for a while it was a day-by-day, relationship-by-relationship decision. I would date. I would kiss (I'm not suggesting kissing is right for everyone). And I would pray.

I would start my prayer as raw as possible and tell God exactly how I was feeling. (Of course, He already knows how we are feeling, but confession brings a sense of humility and opens our hearts to discernment.) And then I would clearly—and with an honest heart—ask Him to give me discernment if I was not acting in a way that was honoring Him.

When it was clear that I was out of line, I repented and asked God to give me the strength to not repeat the behavior. I asked Him to make known the way out of temptation as He had promised (1 Cor. 10:13) so I wouldn't feel trapped in my situation. I knew I couldn't depend on myself to make the right decision in the heat of the moment, so I needed to depend on His exit plan. When the answers back weren't clear, I usually self-reflected and then tried again when I wasn't so emotional. Our emotions can often drown out His voice.

The trend I noticed was that when I was able to put aside my own emotion to hear Him as honestly as I could, those messages were always more discernible. As before, I wrote. I noted in my journal or in my phone the things I heard so that I wouldn't have the option later to say I didn't know. This is one way to live out James 4:17.

4. CHECK YOUR CHOICE OF RELATIONSHIPS; SEEK TRANSPARENCY

As far as relationships, I didn't have all the answers there either, but there were a couple of things that started to build the foundation for what God wanted for me. First was that the man had to be a Christian. The Bible talks a lot about why this is important, but my heart already knew it. If the man I was with didn't love the God who created me and claimed my heart as His own, then how could he love me? I wouldn't be able to even start conversations about how to honor God with someone who didn't know who God was.

Second, the man had to be willing to be my friend before he became my boyfriend. So one tactic I used when meeting a new guy was to tell him that our time together was strictly friendship until we both agreed for it to be something else. That weeded out expectation and pressure and also a lot of men who weren't willing to put effort into having a relationship with me without sex.

Next, as mentioned earlier, I was bold enough to say up front that even if our relationship progressed beyond friendship, I didn't want to have sex before marriage. This always felt like a weighty conversation, but it was another safety measure to weed out those with alternate expectations. I knew once I got beyond all this that someone who was still there would truly be interested in a relationship with me. This was a critical step for me to be able to show God by action, not just word, that I truly did trust Him (James 2:14–26). These conversations were never easy, but they were critical for my not wasting time where God didn't want me to be.

While my communication was usually the first bold step in transparency in a relationship, I learned that it was critical for it to be reciprocated, especially as it applied to "burn territory," to determine if our values were aligned. I started to understand that if a man wasn't willing to talk about his own limitations and temptations openly, that was probably reason enough to stay away. I didn't expect him to have all the answers—I knew I certainly didn't—and even some confusion around the topic seemed normal. But not being willing to talk about it at all is the same as leaving it up to the heat of the moment in the dark, and nothing good ever happens in the dark (Ezek. 8:12) unless you're married!

While these initial steps did weed out many ill-intentioned men, I still dated men who spanned the gamut. This isn't a foolproof way of avoiding fools, but praise be to God, He helped guard me from what and who He was not preparing for me.

When I met Geoff (who was to become my husband), I learned a whole new lesson. Geoff was a believer, passionate about transparency and doing the Word (James 1:22). He was aligned with my values of not having sex before marriage and was honest about his own sense of struggle in that. He was willing to talk openly about us, our temptations, and our individual boundaries for "burn."

But the additional important lesson came because I was truly seeking a God-honoring relationship and held firm to finding it. While I touched briefly on this earlier, it was an eye-opening experience for me. Finally finding a man who put God first (and me second) taught me that this was a relationship among the three of us, so I did not need to carry the burden of these answers on my own. In fact, the more Geoff and I grew in nonsexual intimacy, the more clearly I could discern with him what was off limits and what was not.

Geoff and I talked about this topic frequently, and most of the time our discernment was aligned. It helped to reassure me that I wasn't making up something in my head and that we were both diligently seeking and receiving similar messages. For us, constant communication, seeking discernment, and acknowledging when we were bordering on conviction were our strategies to avoid the burn. Perhaps it goes without saying that it also was incredibly reassuring that God was bringing these messages to us both. He gave us reassurance that He was with us and with our relationship and not against it.

So if you find a man seeking to put God first, your chances are much better that one or both of you will receive conviction if things are going too far. Now I'm not suggesting that you test all the waters to see what the point of conviction is, but God knows your heart. If you know something is sinful for you or your boyfriend, yet you willingly continue to engage in it just because you know we serve a gracious and forgiving God, you've got it all wrong. Jesus makes it clear in John 14:15 when He says, "If you love me, keep my commands."

If we love Him, we will do what He says. It's really that simple. Otherwise, we are proclaiming to love Him but doing something else, which makes us hypocrites and liars. Worse than that, Psalm 66:18 is a powerful reminder of another effect of remaining in our sin: "If I had cherished sin in my heart, the Lord would not have listened." When you are desperately trying to live God's way, the last thing you want is to have Him stop listening or responding to your prayers. Don't cut off the only source of truth and guidance that matters in eternity for some temporary pleasure in the present. Our God also desires transparency.

So if your heart is honestly with Him and you are seeking answers through prayer and studying the Word, you will hear from Him (Deut. 4:29). If the answers are not coming, then you need to be still and know that He is God (Ps. 46:10). Waiting is a great test of your faith. In your waiting, something will be revealed.

5. Submit to the Holy Spirit to Live It Out

Earlier, I referenced how we often underestimate the power of the Holy Spirit. I want to give you a real-life view of what the struggle looked like for me and how the Holy Spirit helped us to persevere. He is the only one who can do it. Even if you faithfully follow the previous four steps, you won't be successful if you don't put this fifth one into practice (John 15:5).

When Geoff and I were courting, we lived three hours apart. Neither of us originally intended to be in a long-distance relationship, but God kept prompting each of us to widen our preferred geographic ranges on eHarmony until we finally crossed into each other's circles. God moved us from friendship to courting quickly after we finally met, and the intention of both toward marriage was clear from the beginning. While we talked on the phone for at least an hour each day, we weren't able to see each other as often as we would have liked. But as the saying goes, absence makes the heart grow fonder. The intense chemistry between us was not something either of us had experienced in any other relationship. The struggle was real, and temptation was ever present as we were falling more and more deeply in love with one another.

There were times when I would literally cry with Geoff, as the screaming in my head, because of what my flesh wanted, was almost unbearable. God used these moments to unexpectedly reassure me that Geoff was the one He wanted for me, because when the burden seemed too great for me to hear God through the noise, Geoff would submit to the Holy Spirit in him to calm the storm in me. He would pray for us and remind me that God loves us enough for us to choose—but that He has a lifetime of blessings in store for us for making the choice for Him. God, through Geoff, would remind me of how far we had come by His grace and strength, including the miracle of even meeting one another at all. God arranged for our meeting and us being together. If He was for us, who could be against us (Rom. 8:31)? Geoff would help me regain my perspective, and slowly the noise in my head would quiet down. Immense gratitude always followed. I thanked God constantly for seeing us through these nights of battling the flesh. I couldn't have done it alone.

Still, one particular evening after we were engaged and the temptation had heightened even further, I was struggling immensely. I desperately wanted to be with my soon-to-be husband, and my flesh felt like I simply could not wait. In the struggle, the Enemy began a great work in my mind, justifying all the actions I wanted to take place because we were engaged, which was "close enough" and therefore would be "understandable." God stepped in to calm the storm, but this time something else followed.

When the storm calmed, my body felt entirely void of sexual desire for a time. This was not something I had experienced with Geoff because of the way God has lined up our compatibility. And the long-distance nature of our relationship only increased our desire when we were together. I knew this sudden and unexplainable shift was not coming from me and certainly was not something that Geoff had done. I was grateful to God for being so effective in calming the storm, but I also knew there was a greater message here for me: a warning.

The warning to me was this: as much as God had blessed Geoff and me with genuine, compatible sexual desire for one another, He could also take it away. Honestly, having struggled with what seemed like a high sex drive most of my life, I am not used to being without it, especially once my passion for someone is fully engaged. Yet for a brief period, at the height of my passion, I was entirely separated from my sex drive. It was as though God had brought me to the peak of the mountain to remind me that I wouldn't be able to breathe the air I was used to unless He made provision for it. This was God's doing, and God's message, God's warning to me to remind me of His control to which I am to be subject. It actually helped me to realize that

God wanted me to cherish the gift of my passion and my desire. As He had given it, He could also take it away.

After sharing my testimony with a friend (once I was married), she was honest and doubtful about her own ability to make it to the altar without having sex with her boyfriend. She said, "That sounds great. I know that's what God wants for me too. I just can't do it." My answer to her, like my answer to you, is that you are 100 percent right.

You can't do it.

Only He can. His Spirit living in you will be the only thing that can empower you to conquer your flesh.

So in that moment, you need to stop what you're doing and get to Him immediately. You need to get yourself and your desires temporarily out of the way, look around to realistically see God's exit strategy for you (1 Cor. 10:13), get somewhere where you can hear God again, and confess what you can't do on your own. If you are close enough to the flame to still feel the heat, you are close enough to still get burned. You need to get out of the driver's seat if you want Him to get in.

If you are a believer in Jesus Christ, your feelings don't define you. When they rise up—no matter how strong—you can acknowledge them and step aside to submit to the power of the Holy Spirit. Feelings can have a place in your life without controlling your actions. The Holy Spirit enables us to do this, even with the most intense feelings. My urgent prayer in moments such as these often sounded something like this: "Lord, You know I can't do this, but I believe You want me to. Give me Your strength, God. Enable me to do what I can't do." And when all else fails, run. Embrace Joseph's strategy when he was lured by Potiphar's wife, and literally run (Gen. 39). God will always provide an escape route.

One benefit of holy living is that you don't have to endure anything on your own. The process of stepping aside to allow the Holy Spirit to do that which you aren't able to do—and don't want to do—is the essence of unity with God. So if you find yourself continually defeated in an area as a Christian, it's likely that you're leaning on your own strength or waiting for your feelings to align to try to find that strength. You can't—and shouldn't try—to do in your own strength that which the Holy Spirit is already prepared to do. He's already got the exact means to do for you what you can't do yourself.

Consider my quick example here to illustrate the point. I'm not exactly a handy woman. I can hang a picture, but I don't have a lot of industrial skills, and I'm not educated when it comes to using power tools or anything like that. I remember once attempting to use sandpaper on a wood project that I now know clearly required an electric sander. When my dad found out what I was doing, he had a great laugh. I was young, naïve, and so determined to complete the task that I was willing to wear out my hands and arms trying to do the work that he already had the perfect tool for. Working in my power and strength led to unnecessary suffering for me and failure in accomplishing my goal. Needless to say, I wasted a lot of time. My daddy had the right tool all along. Sister, step aside and let Him work.

THE CALL TO MARRIAGE

Establishing boundaries in the premarital stage is critical, but honoring God-ordained boundaries is something we are all called to as believers, regardless of our marital status. However, since much of this book is directed to a sister who is likely hoping for or preparing for the stage of marriage, I want to be clear to acknowledge that God has sovereignly designed a unique plan for each of us. The Bible confirms for us that marriage is good, but not everyone is supposed to be married. Genesis 2:18 reads, "It is not good for the man to be alone," yet Jesus also states in Matthew 19:12 that some are not meant to be given in marriage, and "The one who can accept this should accept it." Paul wasn't married, and he viewed that as a gift from God (1 Cor. 7:7). I believe that marriage is a specific call from God as it is a ministry in itself. I also believe it is important for us to do our best to understand if God is calling us to marriage, or if it is our own desire or preference to seek marriage.

Personally, I did want to remarry, but I wasn't sure if it was God's plan for me. I did not want to be alone, but I asked God directly what He wanted for me. I urge you to do the same. I want you to know that I had to get to a raw and lonely place where I was desperate to hear from Him on this. I brought all my passion in the request. I told Him what I wanted with a clean heart (Ps. 51:10) and pure intention. I also told Him that I trusted Him to strengthen and provide for me if remarrying was not in His plan for me.

Lying in bed one night surrounded by the loneliness and desire trying to consume me, I was journaling to Him, pouring out everything that needed to come out of my heart. It was that night that He answered me in a deeply personal way, ensuring me that His plan was for me to remarry and that I needed to be patient in letting Him prepare both me and my future husband. While I didn't have any idea of the timeline for that, His gracious confirmation helped to settle some of my unnecessary anxiety.

I urge you to get desperate enough to seek Him wholeheartedly, as Jeremiah 29:13 says. If you love Him, you can be assured that no matter what His answer, He will make a way, and He will work all of it for your good (Rom. 8:28).

I was married thirty-four months after that confirmation, as He moved me from my previous rebellious burn territory to a passionate and appropriate submission to Him. And with that, I did finally find someone who burned in His passion for me. His name, the only name by which I am saved, is Jesus Christ (Acts 4:12).

CHAPTER 7

Put On, Put Off—Real World Tactics: Sustaining Tools for the Terrain

Not everyone who says to me, "Lord, Lord," will enter the kingdom of heaven, but only the one who does the will of my Father who is in heaven. (Matt. 7:21)

Y ou have read thus far about who I was, how God changed me to desire His ways, and the truth I discovered that allowed me to navigate the boundaries necessary to serve the Lord during a time of singleness. In this chapter I want to share the practical application and strategies to sustain and successfully endure the battle. Our conduct during this time will have a tremendous impact on the suffering or joy we experience in this season.

The Bible places a lot of emphasis on our actions. While we can't be saved by our actions alone, they reveal a great deal about the authenticity of our commitment to Christ. We can't claim to follow Christ and not follow His commands and instruction. That doesn't mean we are perfect at it, but it does mean that we're fully engaged to try to do all He has commanded.

Doing the Word is how we're to show our love for Him (John 14:15), and it's also the means by which we stay clearheaded and ensure that blessings follow. In James, the Bible says:

> But prove yourselves doers of the word, and not merely hearers who delude themselves. For if anyone is a hearer of the word and not a doer, he is like a man who looks at his natural face in a mirror; for once he has looked at himself and gone away, he has immediately forgotten what kind of person he was. But one who looks intently at the perfect law, the law of liberty, and abides by it, not having become a forgetful hearer but an effectual doer, this man will be blessed in what he does.
> (James 1:22–25 NASB)

In my stage of singleness, the last thing I wanted to be was deluded. I wanted to be clearheaded, discerning, wise in my decisions, and obviously, I wanted to be blessed. According to James, without actually doing what the Bible tells us to do, all these are at great risk. Have you ever been so deluded that you forget what your appearance is like? This is hard for most women to perceive, as many of us (myself included) spend a good amount of time preparing our appearance in front of the mirror.

As God's instruction book and love story for humanity, the Bible actually reveals to us who we are in Christ. If we're not fully embracing that in action—even if we read it or listen to it preached—we're missing the best and most life-giving part of being a Christian. Without putting on the Word, we're missing the opportunity to realize Christ's power in us through the power of the Holy Spirit. In other words, we have limited vision, as though the mirror were cracked, fogged, and distorted. Can any sister out there tell me that you enjoy the poor lighting and awkwardly distorted mirrors in some dressing rooms?

Is there any other area of your life in which you would willingly allow distortion?

In my walk as a single woman, I began to understand the importance of following the Bible's direction. Just as I had originally wanted a list of acceptable and unacceptable limits of affection before marriage, I also sought exact direction as to how to stay within those limits. Knowing I couldn't entirely trust myself in the heat of the moment, I wanted a specific strategy as to how to get through it and how to avoid unnecessary struggle before it happened.

I know some would say, "It's simple; just don't be alone with someone in the same room." While that's solid advice, it's not enough for a woman like me who spent much of her time thinking about sex. I needed strategy and tools that extended all the way to my thoughts. So I sought them out. I read a few books that were genuinely helpful, and I read some that weren't. Some gave me new perception on the sacredness of sex and marriage, and that right perspective planted seeds of awe and reverence in me. (Many of these books, with some of the important answers I found from these sources, are highlighted in the next chapter.)

My new perception of the spiritual importance of sex and the reverence it deserved was the foundation. In locating the strategy to implement it, my wise counselor was the apostle Paul. In many of Paul's letters, such as Corinthians, Philippians, Colossians, and Galatians, he gives straightforward advice for biblical living by contrasting what we need to start doing with what we need to stop doing: the "putting on" and the "putting off." One example of this wise instruction is found in Ephesians 4:22–24:

> You were taught, with regard to your former way
> of life, to put off your old self, which is being
> corrupted by its deceitful desires; to be made new in
> the attitude of your minds; and to put on the new
> self, created to be like God in true righteousness
> and holiness.

It's imperative to put on and put off simultaneously, as combining them is what makes this strategy effective. You may be able to temporarily stop a bad habit, but without replacing it with something better, you'll be tempted to return to the habit to fill the void.

If you decide to stop cursing, for example, that's certainly a good thing, and you'll find plenty of scriptural support confirming the importance of wise and holy speech. But perhaps you go a step further and take a vow of silence. You determine that you won't speak to anyone, not because God demands this, but out of fear that you'll accidentally curse. That vow may prohibit you from cursing, but you'll also miss sharing the good news. If you don't put on the ability to speak wholesome words, you'll miss sharing your testimony with someone who needs to hear it, and you'll stay quiet when you see someone in danger. You won't curse, but you'll miss some holy opportunities to witness to the world and even to potentially save someone from harm.

Or what if you go on a diet and put off junk food, but forget to put on healthy eating? You'd starve! This may seem like a simple example, but God's instructions are often much simpler than we make them out to be. If we put off sin, we're to fill that void by putting on that which is holy. God doesn't want us to be empty and fearful in the pursuit of holiness. He wants us to be active, wise, and productive and to walk in the truth of His love. This is a lifelong process. Biblical living is an ongoing sanctification and consecration process that comes through the active discipleship of life in the Spirit and in God's Word. We don't put on righteous living and put off sinful behavior in a single act. It's a daily choice to pursue the narrow path.

> Therefore everyone who hears these words of mine and puts them into practice is like a wise man who built his house on the rock.
> (Matt. 7:24)

THE BENEFITS OF PUTTING ON AND PUTTING OFF

The benefits of the put-on-put-off strategy extend beyond corrective actions and behavioral limitations. Remember that I needed a strategy that would address the core level of my thoughts? God's got that covered too. The Biblical Counseling Foundation (BCF) points out:

> As you stop (put off) the old continuing pattern of
> sin, and begin (put on) the new practice of righ-
> teousness and holiness, you are renewed in the
> spirit of your mind.[3]
> (Rom. 6:11–14, 16–23; 12:1–2; Eph. 4:22–24;
> Phil. 2:12–13; Col. 3:5–17; 2 Tim. 2:19)

Most of our problems are rooted in wrong attitudes and thinking, so this strategy is powerful because it pinpoints and removes the causes of wrong thinking. It doesn't mask symptoms or cover sin; it addresses sin at its source. In other words, the put-on-put-off strategy is proactive rather than reactive. According to Scripture, this process renews our mind. It's the holy equivalent of a complete system reset to help us naturally align with God's intent and purpose for us. With a renewed mind, you're not struggling to desire and exhibit godly behavior, so it's much easier to put on and keep on. Sisters, this strategy not only sets our feet to walk on the right path, but it also sets our heart on a path to enjoy it.

So let's see what put-ons and put-offs are most critical in our pursuit of sexual purity, starting with our perception of outward beauty and the contrast between

---

3. John C. Broger, developer, *Self-Confrontation: A Manual for In-Depth Biblical Discipleship* (Indio, CA: Biblical Counseling Foundation, 1991).

isolation and discipleship, and from there moving on to hot topics like sexual temptation and masturbation.

PUT ON THE BEAUTY OF GOD; PUT OFF THE WORLDLY STANDARDS

My sister, it's inevitable that the closer you get to Jesus in your walk, the more you're going to be separate from this world and its standards of what's right, lovely, and attractive. To pursue God, you simply can't stay in two worlds. Part of this process will be to grow to understand what God considers lovely and to start to take off, or put off, that which He doesn't.

I encourage you to read for yourself the following Scriptures that reference traits and characteristics that describe a human reflection of God's beauty. These should be our defining guidelines for what we need to put on and put off:

- 1 Peter 3:3–4
- 1 Timothy 2:9–10
- 1 Timothy 3:11
- Proverbs 11:22
- Proverbs 31:10-31
- 1 Samuel 16:7
- 2 Corinthians 4:16
- Psalm 34:5

- Ecclesiastes 3:11
- Colossians 3:12

CAN I DRESS SEXY AND HOLY AT THE SAME TIME?

I know this is a controversial question. I personally believe the answer is yes, but I'll explain why. To me, sexiness is more of an attitude, an inner character, than it is about outward appearance. We've all witnessed beautiful women dressed provocatively, but the moment they open their mouths, they kill all the outward beauty. On the other hand, we also have met women who by worldly standards aren't so lovely, but whose character and inner beauty make them breathtakingly beautiful, powerfully overshadowing their outward physical appearance. Although we can invest a great deal of time in making ourselves appear beautiful on the outside, that can be ruined in a moment by foolishness seeping out from the inside.

So I'd like to make a clear distinction. I don't think you can dress *provocatively* and holy at the same time (unless the only man seeing you is your husband). Purposely provocative dress in public is eye-catching and attention seeking, no matter how you cut it. And it's not attractive, especially not to a godly man. Don't believe me? Check out Proverbs 11:22: "Like a gold ring in a pig's snout is a beautiful woman who shows no discretion."

If you're purposely calling a man's attention to your body, then you're not calling him to your spirit. As a sister in Christ, you're doing that man a great disservice by getting his attention off Jesus. Now to be clear, that doesn't excuse any sinful behavior on a man's part just because you have dressed provocatively. The Bible says we're each responsible for our own behavior and will be held accountable for it. But you would do well to not purposely place any of your brothers in temptation. You know when you look hot, and so do they. And they most definitely aren't immune to it just because you're in church looking hot. (They may, in fact, be even more susceptible there.)

What I'm suggesting here is a balance. Don't go out of your way to purposely wear clothes that are three sizes too big because you're afraid that someone will see a curve. Find clothes that compliment you without showing you off. You should feel great in what you wear. You can be fun in what you wear. You can definitely even be trendy in what you wear. But you can't be worldly. There's a big difference. Worldliness is an attitude that caters to the sin nature of the world and man's perception, more than God's, of what is attractive. Holiness and worldliness never go together.

The combination of godly confidence, genuine humility, and holy identification is one of the sexiest traits you can wear. And, sister, you can be in a turtleneck, long skirt, and a head covering without an inch of skin showing, but if you're rocking that inner beauty, there will be a palpable sexiness about you. It's eye-catching, not-of-this-world kind of startling. And that's the way God has intended to set you apart. He wants to catch others' eyes with His holiness in you. And God's beauty shines a light that far outweighs any notion of our perception of sexiness.

Consider this also. If God has a marriage planned for your future, then your body is meant to be a gift to your future husband. It's been designed with him in mind! It's much more exciting to get a gift fully wrapped and prepared in nice wrapping paper without holes and tears that reveal what's inside. And if that gift were meant for him, do you really think he would want others peeking through the revealing parts of that package? The reveal for him will be even more magnificent and exciting when he's the only one who gets it. The choices you make now are preparing this gift for him in that moment.

Put off immodesty. Put on a loving-your-neighbor attitude that takes your brothers into account. God's standard says that we don't need elaborate hairstyles, fancy jewels, or fine clothes, but we should shine from an inner beauty—a "gentle and quiet spirit" (1 Peter

3:3–4). Let the refined, conservative gentle and quiet spirit of a Christ-grounded woman be the sexiness you wear in bold confidence. And trust God to do the rest.

LIKE ATTRACTS LIKE

It's often said that opposites attract, and that may be true in certain circumstances. Certainly opposites can complement each other well, assuming they're well grounded in the major areas. My husband and I are opposites in small ways, and those things balance us out as a couple and as parents. But, sister, if you're a woman of God looking for a man of God, you can't justify major differences in values with the phrase *opposites attract*. In other words, you can't brush aside areas of sin as insignificant because you have different opinions about them. Your opinion of what is sinful doesn't actually matter, and neither does his. The only opinion about sin that matters is God's, so you must agree that God's Word settles any differences between you two.

There are many examples in Scripture that illustrate the principle that we become like those we hang around with, emulate, and follow. The more time we spend with them, the more we become like them. Jesus instructed the disciples to follow Him for that very reason. The purpose of our consecration is to conform us to His image. So even if we begin as disciples who aren't at all like Him, essentially His opposites, we're on a lifelong path to mirror His character and become like Him. And this is just what happened to the apostles.

So why am I referencing this within the "beauty" section of this chapter? Because the world will tell you that you need to appeal to a man's worldly nature to catch his eye. And I want you to hear that you cannot attract a like-minded man of God while acting like a woman ruled by her flesh or swayed by worldly philosophy. Even though we know we shouldn't dress provocatively, it's easy to feel beat down by worldly pressure, tempted by the lust of the flesh, and confused by the twisted logic that surrounds us. We can believe the distortion that tries to claim that what God says is wrong may in fact be okay. That's actually the oldest trick in the Book (see Genesis). In other words, the world, Satan, and your flesh will tell you that even a godly man is a man and you need to appeal to him as a man—with provocative dress, sexy speech, seductive moves, and loose boundaries.

Sister, real life isn't some Christian version of the nineties movie *Pretty Woman* or some other highly exaggerated fairy tale. Only in a completely fictional world can a woman behave like a prostitute while her knight in shining armor—who happens to be a rich godly man in training to be a pastor—pulls his sports car over to her corner to rescue her because he sees her inner beauty. (Yet some of us still think that way!) That man, if he's really a man of God, should avoid women who act that way. And he definitely shouldn't be in the club acting foolish with you. I've found a great deal of truth in the saying, "The way you get them is the way you lose them." If you've attracted your man by appealing to his sensual nature, then don't you think another woman will have the same power over him? A man so vulnerable to sensuality isn't the kind of man who can lead you well. He's not wearing his spiritual armor and will be weak in this and other areas. This isn't the kind of man you want. Nancy Kaser, author of *CROWN: 30 Wife-Changing Lessons*, encourages modesty by pointing out, "You can tell what kind of fish you're trying to catch by the kind of bait you use!"

Any man God would give you as a husband wouldn't be attracted to you because of your efforts to seduce him with worldly means of beauty. Like attracts like. The Holy Spirit in a godly man will be attracted to the Holy Spirit shining through you—not some distraction from that.

Sometimes that attraction is something God grows in His timing, not a love-at-first-sight sort of situation. It's wise not to place too much emphasis on sensual attraction one way or another, especially initially. The Spirit is what you need to have in common. If that man is meant to become your spouse, God will ensure the yielding of not just hearts, but minds and bodies in that same direction together. He's a God of order and peace, so if there's serious opposition between you and your intended spouse, it's likely that He's not the one bringing you together. God creates intentional complements within marriage, not opponents. Put on the beauty of God and see who He brings toward you.

Put On Community and Discipleship; Put Off Isolation

When I was single, I struggled with depression even after I was saved. I experienced times of great joy and rejoicing, but the "old man" that was used to being emotionally led was fighting hard for survival. Anytime I didn't hold on to and cling to God's truth that the "old man" had died and that I was actually free from my past shackles of sin (Rom. 6:6), I would find plenty of reason to sink into depression and further fuel it with isolation. Without the light of other believers around, it became increasingly dark. Indeed, isolation is the setting for Satan to run wild, because you may not be able to see what he's doing in the dark.

During one such time of depression, a friend suggested that I do some volunteer work. I remember feeling angry at her suggestion. How in the world was she expecting that I was going to help someone else when I couldn't even help myself? I rationalized my attitude by claiming that I could actually do harm if I tried to serve others in their time of need from a place of deficit myself. I convinced myself that I couldn't give until my "bucket" was full and I had something to give. Sisters, while this bucket notion does have some validity, I caution you not to twist its meaning into something it's not, as I did.

When we feel like our bucket isn't full, it's because we're looking to the wrong thing to fill the bucket. But the good news is that if you're a Christian, your bucket is already full, and you have all you need to give to others, no matter how you feel. The proof? "We love because he first loved us" (1 John 4:19).

Jesus filled the romance and love buckets for all believers for all time with His sacrifice on the cross. If your bucket feels empty, consider what you think would help fill it. Would it be one of the eternal provisions of Christ, or would it be a temporary lust of life such as a fabulous husband, new car, better job, or bigger house? Are you looking in the right direction?

I'm grateful to tell you that I overcame the lie that convinced me that I wasn't able to serve and to give to others because I didn't feel fulfilled as an unmarried woman. My friend's advice was absolutely spot-on. She saw that I was entirely focused on myself and that I was actually missing out on the blessing of service and the adjustment in perspective that comes with serving. The time of my greatest need was the time when it was actually ideal for me to be giving to others. If Jesus loved you enough to die for your sins and save you for eternity, then you are loved enough in the present to share His love with others in your community. And, sister, I'm going to encourage you to find another sister right now and put this into practice. Paul conveys the importance of us discipling one another, even among different generations:

> Likewise, teach the older women to be reverent in the way they live, not to be slanderers or addicted to much wine, but to teach what is good. Then they can urge the younger women to love their husbands and children, to be self-controlled and pure, to be busy at home, to be kind, and to be subject to their husbands, so that no one will malign the word of God. (Titus 2:3–5)

As much as I love the thought of calling up a girlfriend right now and going shopping together to talk about Jesus in between ice cream and soda, I know it's got to be more than that. We can't ignore the critical marching orders we have been given that need to be consistent in our time with her, no matter what we're doing. Older women are to be sober and wise with words, especially in how they talk about others (not slanderous). They're to take the initiative in teaching the younger women how to:

- Love their husbands (directing that attention to Jesus if they're unmarried)
- Love their children in servant leadership
- Demonstrate self-control by seeing our example
- Take care of their home, considering all that God has entrusted to them
- Focus outwardly, as the mind naturally wants to focus on self
- Be kind, even in an unkind world
- Submit to their husband and to Jesus, who is the ultimate focus of our submission

And younger women are to seek out older women to disciple them in this very way. Why is it so important to check these boxes on our ice cream date? It's so "no one will malign the word of God." I'm sure if you're like me, you read over that part quickly, but I want to urge you to take a second look at the wording in this verse.

Most of us are familiar with the term *malignancy*. It's the dreaded word none of us want to hear from a doctor, as it indicates the presence of a dangerous form of cancer. A malignancy is a toxic community of cells gone wild. In our bodies this abnormal, unnatural growth of our cells can quickly lead to death. In the Christian walk, it's the abnormal, unnatural twisting of God's Word that justifies sin. Maligning and twisting the Word of God is a cancer-like sin. And what are the wages of sin? Death

(Rom. 6:23). If you're not convinced that maligning the Word of God is an incredibly serious sin, consider that it's one of the last things Jesus warns us about as the Bible closes. Some of the last verses in the final chapter of Revelation say:

> I warn everyone who hears the words of the prophecy of this scroll: If anyone adds anything to them, God will add to that person the plagues described in this scroll. And if anyone takes words away from this scroll of prophecy, God will take away from that person any share in the tree of life and in the Holy City, which are described in this scroll. (Rev. 22:18–19)

Have you ever told your kids one last thing before you left home? Or have you received that last instruction before your mom or boss left? We all know how serious that last piece of instruction is. It's intended to linger so it makes an unforgettable impression. God's Word is to be taken as seriously as life and death. It's not to be forgotten or taken lightly.

Seeking a godly discipleship relationship with a sister and leading by example isn't just obedience to the Great Commission (Matt. 28:16–20). It's an antioxidant that prevents the malignancy that occurs when God's Word is rejected, misused, or treated as anything but holy and sacred. Consider how often we're warned to guard against cancer in our bodies. Guarding against cancer in our heart and soul is even more important because our bodies are temporary, but our souls are eternal. This time in which you're single—and your attention may be less divided—is a great opportunity to give discipleship your full attention.

This is your take-home assignment: Go seek another sister today—this very day. Text her, call her, or email her and ask her when you can get together. Find out what you can pray about for her. You can be sure that something she's struggling with will relate to an experience you've already had, so you will likely have some helpful advice. Bless her with the presence of a godly, self-controlled, sober woman who speaks with wisdom so that she knows they do exist. (You may be the only example in her life.) Teach her what you're learning in this season of your life, even if you don't have it all figured out. Help her understand what it means to guard her heart, take her focus off herself, and understand and apply God's Word appropriately. Then inspire in her the desire to go do the same with a younger sister. The Great Commission is more about living the gospel with others where they are than the need to travel somewhere to carry it out.

Seek opportunities to get to know people who have much more serious problems than you, and visit them for an hour or two. You don't need to serve soup (although that's helpful), and you don't need to walk down streets to pass out socks and toothbrushes to the homeless (although that's a wonderful thing to do too). Sometimes you just need to take time with someone to let them know that they're heard and that there's hope because they're loved. It's important—vitally important—to feed them, clothe them, and provide for other needs if you're able. But it's equally important, if not more so, to point them to sustaining spiritual nourishment, which is living water for their soul (John 4:10). Let them know that, like you, they don't have to feel that their bucket isn't full, because God, the source of love (1 John 4:8), has already secured, filled, and provided provision for you and for them to last for all eternity no matter what the temporary circumstances look like. Don't isolate yourself, and don't walk past those near you who are trying to isolate themselves. Be someone's antioxidant by covering them in truth, because you're equipped to do so this very day (2 Peter 1:3).

One last note about isolation. Isolation keeps us from accountability, and accountability is one of the most important elements of Christian growth. Yes, we're ultimately accountable to God for all we do, but having godly Christian accountability is one of the most critical aspects of fellowship. It helps us weed out deception, and godly accountability partners will often be used to speak His truth in a way we can hear it.

PUT ON HOLY SURROUNDINGS AND REMINDERS; PUT OFF SEXUAL TEMPTATIONS AND UNHOLY JUSTIFICATIONS

Every night I pray Proverbs 4:23 over my boys: "Above all else, guard your heart, for everything you do flows from it." Sister, especially during a time of singleness, it's critically important for you to guard your life by standing guard over your heart. Our heart is impacted quickest through our senses: that which we see, hear, taste, and touch. What we surround ourselves with affects us whether we expect it to or not. What we allow near us may unexpectedly linger even when we have sent it packing. I tell my boys frequently that we can't "unsee" something.

For women, we often can't "unhear" anything either. (Have you ever been in an argument with someone and brought up something they said from five years ago to see the look of shock on their face?) Our senses are extremely powerful. Remember that the serpent got to Eve through her senses as he redefined what was good, beautiful, and pleasurable. Eve's heart was originally with God because she was without sin, but with a subtle yet powerful appeal to her senses, Satan won her over. In other words, that which appeals to your hearing, sight, and sense of taste, touch, and smell may be the quickest way to target your heart. And when your heart is targeted, so is your very life. The purpose of this section isn't to convince you to become a good Christian girl by listening only to gospel music or reading only Christian books. It's much deeper than that. It's about protecting your very life.

You may have heard that men are more visually stimulated than women, and although powerful visual stimulation isn't limited to men, there is much evidence that what we women hear can impact us even more powerfully. Have you ever been in a store when a song came on that unexpectedly brought up an intense memory of an event in your past? Author Shannon Ethridge confirms that music is indeed a very powerful sensual tool, especially for those women who are "typically more stimulated by what they hear than by what they see."[4]

The power of a sweet-talking man telling us everything we ever wanted to hear is dangerous, and if not guarded against, can be like a toxin injected in your veins, changing you from the inside out before you even know it. But this isn't just about guarding against the sweet-sounding man with sinister intentions. Sister, you need to guard your ears just as much against that fellow

---

4. Shannon Ethridge, *The Fantasy Fallacy: Exposing the Deeper Meaning Behind Sexual Thoughts* (Nashville Thomas Nelson, 2012), 41–42.

sister who constantly bad-mouths her husband and justifies her own sinful actions by his behavior.

You need to guard yourself against so-called Christian messages that contain tones of self-love, self-righteousness, feminism, or any other "ism" that isn't of Christ. "Isms" don't reflect Christ; holiness does. You need to guard your ears from music that encourages you to cross any boundary that you wouldn't cross in front of your grandmother or grandfather. You even need to guard your ears from famous Christian pep talkers who do more self-promotion than truth-promotion. These messages plant seeds that grow like relentless weeds in your spirit and torment you into believing that you should be somewhere other than where God has you right in this season.

Guard your eyes well. Don't linger in front of the shelf with the romance novel covers featuring men who look sweaty and in need of a girl like you. Get rid of pictures of old boyfriends. What holy reason could there be for holding on to these? And I plead with you to consider refraining from (at least most) R-rated movies. R-rated films have much looser boundaries than they once did, and there really is no need to take the chance of seeing something that will haunt you when you need to be carefully guarded instead.

Pornography is totally off limits as well. Author and speaker Greg Speck does a phenomenal job of explaining both the physical and spiritual impacts of pornography, and I highly recommend his books. This isn't an area to dabble in. I guarantee it will never show you how to be a better lover, teach you what men really want, or improve your relationship. They're all lies from the Enemy to entice you. Porn is unadulterated distortion that goes entirely against God's holy design for sex. If you find yourself caught in a stronghold, address it immediately and find a strong Christian friend or mentor who will keep you biblically accountable.

Was I pure in all these areas prior to my marriage? Absolutely not. I can say all this confidently because I explored these outlets and suffered all the consequences that come with them. Years later I can still easily recall disturbing images that I subjected myself to in justifying my "freedom" to watch porn, read romance or explicit novels, or even, twice, go to a strip club just to experience it for myself. If it were possible, I would pay to remove these past memories. Even now, when I don't quickly take these thoughts captive and cast them off, they can still entrap and imprison me and all my freedom.

Consider what happens when you see something sensual. Your senses (your eyes) have allowed the image to enter your mind, and it lingers. The sensual has potentially moved you to emotion, action, or even momentary fantasy; thus your heart has now been engaged. Once your heart is engaged, your mind starts strategizing to continue the pursuit. The execution of that plan often involves the body. And with this process, beginning with the heart (see what Jesus says in Matthew 5:28), the journey continues until you've impacted your very soul.

But there is good news. Even if you've skipped the first critical step of guarding your heart, there's still hope and a way out of the sin. Before you proceed to action, you first have to engage your mind.

Your mind is like a highway with two lanes and a shoulder, and you get to choose which lane to travel in. You can keep driving in your lane toward the sin, or you can pull over to the shoulder to reassess.

We've all been in that fast lane where nobody is willing to take their time. Our mind has decided on a destination, and it's full-speed ahead to get there. There's the slow lane where you may take a little more time to consider your destination while moving toward it. (Be careful with this!) And, thank God, there's the shoulder where you can pull over to carefully evaluate what you're doing and where you're going. The shoulder is where you pause to take thoughts captive.

The thoughts are the fuel in the car, and engaging them will push you toward your destination regardless of whether or not it's a holy one. Once our hearts are moved, our minds drive. If you don't pull over to take the thoughts captive, you might not even realize that you've given up complete control of the wheel. This isn't about controlling your life; it's about being intentional with your choices to pursue and remain on the path of holiness. Put off careless and irrational choices and put on intentionality. If you're not driving, who is?

The mind presents a powerful intersection that determines the next step of body and soul impact. And masturbation presents a key example of this.

MASTURBATION

This is one topic we don't typically hear about in sermons on Sunday. Unless you're in a discipleship class with established, trusted relationships among group members or in a conversation with a close friend, you're probably not hearing about it too often. At a peak in my sexuality and newly single, I searched thoroughly for answers on this topic. I talked to people, I consulted Christian counselors, I read books, and I referenced the Bible. (The Bible doesn't specifically refer to masturbation, but it does speak to several aspects directly related to it, such as self-control and sexual purity.)

I consistently found that the topic of masturbation was difficult and complicated to discuss, even in Christian circles. I don't think that the church is avoiding this topic because it's not important to God. I think it's being avoided because there's a lot of confusion about how to talk about it. But we can't continue to avoid sensitive topics when we disciple. In areas where things may be slightly unclear, it's even more important for us as a body to examine the Scripture with a sound mind and to help one another hear God's voice above the others.

THE IMPLICATIONS AND IMPACT OF MASTURBATION

I've heard people simplify and make light of the topic of masturbation because it's so commonplace. Some Christians claim that because it's not listed as something strictly forbidden in the Bible, it probably isn't a big deal one way or another. But if, as Christians, our bodies belong to the Lord (1 Cor. 6:19–20), there isn't any way to isolate the effects of what we do with our bodies. The impact of masturbation is one that goes all the way to the core of our relationship with God.

Even though we may not be physically engaging with another person in the moment as with other sexual activity, masturbation still engages our heart, mind, and soul. If our heart has been affected (often signified by shifts in emotion, desire, and interest), our mind has likely moved to planning, strategy, and execution—and we can be assured that body and soul impact are next. If we haven't appropriately taken ungodly thoughts captive, we've entered dangerous landscape where sin and shame can quickly take root. (Remember what Jesus said about committing adultery in Matthew 5:28.) We cannot remain in sin and simultaneously be in close pursuit of God.

And so we begin this topic in the same place we should for all others: Jesus.

In Matthew 22:37–40, Jesus said all the law and prophets could be summed up by two commands: love God and love others. Here's the simple answer to masturbation, and it's the same answer as to any of our other behaviors: We shouldn't do anything that prevents us from loving God with all our heart, mind, body, and soul.

Consider this. Aside from the larger boundaries provided by the Ten Commandments, if we actually had an explicit list of every behavior that we should or should not do, I'm certain that we could still find a way to do even the acceptable behaviors in an ungodly and sinful way. Perhaps there were some things, such as masturbation, that weren't specifically addressed by name in Scripture because they were already addressed when Jesus said for us to love Him beyond even ourselves. Perhaps the answer really is reflective of a need to bring our hearts, not a list, to the Savior to reconcile with His desire for us. If we bring our hearts fully to Him on this topic, then we certainly don't need to drag along a chain of unnecessary emphasis with it.

While it's not to be taken lightly, too many of us have also gone in the opposite direction and attached an unholy weight to masturbation with shame, condemnation, isolation, and confusion. But I can tell you that my God doesn't speak on those terms. We don't need to put more emphasis on this topic than on other areas of holiness. For Christians, decisions regarding our behavior come down to the following biblical principles:

- We must love the Lord our God with all our heart, soul, and mind. (Matt. 22:37)
- We must love our neighbor as ourselves. Our neighbor includes everyone, even our enemies. (Matt. 22:39; 5:44)
- We shouldn't allow anything to master us if we have made Jesus our Lord. (1 Cor. 6:12)
- Sin separates us from God. (Isa. 59:2)
- Sexual sin is the only sin against our own body. These consequences occur deeply, affecting not just our body, but our soul, and can impact us for years, sometimes for a lifetime. (1 Cor. 6:18)
- We're expected to fully repent (turn from) and confess our sin with a pure heart, including asking forgiveness of others we have harmed with our offense. (Matt. 5:23–24; Psa. 32:1–5)

Putting these principles into practice means that if you can't masturbate remaining faithful to your covenant with God (and your spouse if you are already married), then you shouldn't masturbate. If you can't masturbate without coveting or dishonoring others in thought, word, or deed, you shouldn't masturbate. If you can't masturbate without losing the ability to stop at any time that God says so, then you shouldn't masturbate. Yes, that may leave you on a very narrow path, but Jesus calls us to walk the narrow path (Matt. 7:13). True discipleship isn't for the faint of heart. It requires us to bring all our heart, mind, understanding, and desire to the throne and let Him change and mold it as He sees fit.

My opinion on masturbation has changed significantly since I got saved. In talking with others and in researching the topic, I have found some aspects that have impacted me greatly and have brought me once more to a clearer understanding of the importance of yielding my body to the Lord. The closer I've grown to God, the more I've come to realize that masturbation is an issue reflective of our heart, not just our body.

The undeniable problem with masturbation is the high risk associated with it. Our flesh becomes driven and fueled by our senses or thoughts, and most of the time, if we're honest, those thoughts aren't likely yielding to Christ first. Like driving fast, masturbation may cater to our desire at the time, but we might not arrive at our destination safely. We may be hurt in the process, and we may hurt others as well (if we're lusting after someone who isn't our spouse, for example).

The other issue with masturbation is that it provides a place for sexual engagement without the necessity of a spouse. If God has reserved sex for the marital bed, justifying sexual engagement through masturbation outside the marital bed is an unquestionably gray area.

If you're still not convinced that masturbation is risky business, consider that research shows that when you get used to bringing yourself to orgasm, it may be more difficult to reach orgasm by your spouse. Your solo activity may also decrease your interest in regular engagement with your spouse as well. One thing I know for sure is that you don't want anything to interfere with the ecstasy that God will bring you in blessed, holy sex within marriage. And you definitely don't want to mess up your wedding night.

During the process of finishing this manuscript, I met with one of my peer reviewers over breakfast at a local restaurant to get her input on the book. When this topic came up, we both blushed a little trying to figure out ways to discuss this section discreetly while other diners sat close by. We decided to refer to it as "cooking" rather than masturbating, and we both had some good laughs elaborating on the analogy. The analogy actually proved really effective, though, as she pointed out that if you get used to only cooking by yourself for yourself, you will eventually come up with a recipe that you may not want anyone else to mess with. Think about it. If you've mastered your favorite recipe (in this case, bringing yourself to orgasm) exactly to your personal preferences, you may be less likely to believe that someone else is going to pull it off with the same success. You may also be less interested in trying their recipe when it's different from your established one. The hilarious cooking analogy reminded me once again that masturbation creates a solo event out of something that God truly intended to be a shared event between husband and wife.

Additionally, contrary to the belief that we can relieve built-up sexual tension with masturbation, studies show that it's an artificial and temporary satisfaction that only yields increased frustration and desire as it continues. Like anything else that doesn't provide lasting satisfaction, it's easy to seek more in an effort to satisfy what becomes an endless appetite for fulfillment. That's how addictions and strongholds develop. An effective way to gauge your heart on this issue is to honestly check your reaction to the thought of never masturbating again. Consider your immediate and initial reaction, any emotions that rise with it, and the potential causes behind those reactions. Masturbation can become an idol just as easily as anything else.

Since I've learned the implications and impact that it has on us on every level, including in our relationship with God, my position is that engaging in masturbation is not a worthwhile risk. Much good can come out of a decision to refrain from masturbation, and no harm can come from that decision. Much harm can come from a decision to masturbate if it means you're in sin to do so. A heart that is willing to risk sin is a heart that needs greater revelation of how worthy God is, so as not to risk the separation sin provides.

I've placed this topic within the chapter "Put On, Put Off" because I am suggesting putting off masturbation and putting on some really great distraction in its place. I've learned that victory in this area, as in any other battle of the flesh, is only possible by the empowerment of and submission to the Holy Spirit. If you're ready to take this step, be closely aware of the circumstances that regularly align to influence you to struggle most in this area. Is there a particular time of day? A particular temptation which you face routinely? The process of both putting off and putting on something else is such a powerful tool for this particular struggle. Prepare ahead of time to consider what else you can purposely fill your time with and how you can guard your heart and spirit during the times that you anticipate facing temptation. Make sure what you put on is something that does not hinder you in other areas, but rather adds joy, edification, and health to your routine. Be creative with this. You don't have anything to lose pursuing something else to fill your time, and you may discover a way to automatically make room for some other hobby or pursuit you've been considering anyway.

In summary, if you're a Christian, your body doesn't belong to you (1 Cor. 6:19–20). It has been bought at a price, and any decision you make regarding it needs to be yielded to the One who created it. Evaluate the six biblical principles listed previously in this section. If you're single and masturbating, you need to do some really honest reflection to consider your heart's position on the sin you may be risking. And if you're married and doing it, your body belongs to God *and your spouse*, so anything related to sexual activity should be shared, discussed, and agreed upon. I'd also recommend checking out Greg Speck's discussion of this topic in his book *Sex: It's Worth Waiting For.*

PUT ON HIS JOY AND PEACE; PUT OFF BITTERNESS AND EXPECTATION

I remember when I was single how difficult it was to go to church and see happily married couples holding hands during the sermon. I had missed a holy connection with my first husband, and since I got saved, I recognized that connection as the most important thing I wanted in a future relationship. Going to church by myself with those couples around me continuously reminded me of what I didn't have and may never have. It was a constant battle of my mind to stay focused in church.

How could I have dealt with this? I could have stopped going to church. That was the easiest solution and one I seriously considered. Or I could have watched church online from the convenience of my home. Consider the heart, mind, body, and soul connection again. Look what occurred in progression from me feeling bad about not being one of those couples holding hands to the temptation to not go to church. My heart was moved because I wasn't guarding it well. This was my first major problem. My mind was then moved to recognize a problem (since my feelings claimed that there was one) and began to strategize how to deal with the problem. If I hadn't been careful, the next step would have been that my body didn't leave the house on Sunday morning if I rationalized enough to just watch church remotely from home. This would have damaged me spiritually because the fellowship of God's people, live worship, and Holy Spirit movement feeds the soul. While I'm grateful online church is an option for certain circumstances, we can't rationalize this as equivalent to fellowshipping with God's people in person. In fact, I think it's dangerous to think we can choose to remain in isolation from God's people and maintain proper worship (Heb. 10:25).

The Enemy appealed to my senses (in this case through my eyes) and targeted my heart (feelings of loneliness), which moved my mind to strategize (fix the problem) and take me on the road toward body and soul impact. But was it really the Enemy? We give Satan too much credit. He's not all powerful, all knowing, or omnipresent. He has no ability to create. In fact, his tactics are old and worn out. He can do nothing but recycle old tricks. But his targets (looking in the mirror as I say this) are generally weak and unguarded, so even dull weapons can be effective. My pastor, James Betner, used to say, "If the devil ain't bothering you, it's probably because you're walking with him."

Sister, the "lust of the flesh, the lust of the eyes, and the pride of life" (1 John 2:16) weren't created by the Enemy. They were a result of sin entering the world. The Enemy doesn't need a high-powered weapon to get you to a place where you are joyless, frustrated, and bitter. All he needs to do is observe you choosing to live in this sinful, fallen world unguarded, and he can pretty much check that box for you for the day. Our own focus, not the Enemy, is to blame for some of our vulnerability, and definitely for our lack of joy.

So the good news is that it's entirely your choice to live in joy and peace or in bitterness and expectation. If you're focused on yourself, you can be certain that the latter will be the case because everything you see and hear in this world will tell you that you don't have enough to be satisfied. But if you're focused on Jesus and you commit to adopting David's declaration in Psalm 23:1

(NLT), "The Lord is my shepherd; I have all that I need," then the guard on your heart is firm and solid. God's Word is powerful. Keep His Word as the guard, and walk in holy, righteous behavior, because you know you can through His strength. You have activated the strongest armor available to guard your heart: the breastplate of righteousness (Eph. 6:10–18).

Perhaps you know all this. You have the armor of God memorized, you know the importance of it, you know how to pursue holy living, and you know why you should. But you're just tired. You're tired of life seeming so hard and the armor feeling so heavy. You're tired of waiting, and you feel like you're running out of strength. I know exactly what you're talking about. I've been there more times than I can count. And that's where the mystery of what I would call the hidden weapon of joy comes into play.

> Do not grieve, for the joy of the LORD is your strength. (Neh. 8:10)

Friend, you can put on all your armor and sit on your couch, never leaving your house because you're too tired to walk. What good have you done in this day to glorify God? It simply won't do. The Christian walk isn't a solo event and it's not a static event. It's a walk. You're to get up and put on that armor and go into the ends of the earth to do the will of the Father. What's your strength? Joy. The simple and necessary choice of joy.

Choosing joy isn't a burden, and it's not complicated. You don't need to rationalize your circumstance or your feelings to convince yourself that they're suddenly pleasant. If that were the case, you wouldn't need to choose joy because it would naturally follow. And you don't need to ignore your current circumstance or feelings. Instead, acknowledge them, nod your head at them recognizing their presence, tell them to sit down, and ask joy to stand up. Choose to give joy the microphone so she can be louder than the other voices in the room that have well-prepared arguments for you to be self-focused, hurting, depressed, bitter, unsatisfied, and joyless. Don't let them take the mic back from joy. They'll try, but it's your choice. If the Lord is Lord in your life, then they aren't.

You just need to get out of the way to allow His joy to take over. And when this happens, you'll be refueled. If nothing else comes to your heart and mind, I promise that you can find joy in the fact that He has overcome whatever you are facing, that it's temporary, and that this suffering doesn't compare to the glory that is to come (John 16:33; 2 Cor. 4:17; Rom. 8:18). No circumstance you're facing can change any of that, which means that nothing and no one can steal your joy (unless you let them) because it originates from His permanently secured victory.

What if I told you that the season you're in right now is not a detour? Can a detour be considered a detour if it's actually part of the journey? Wouldn't it be easier to feel joyful if you knew it wasn't a detour? Can you be certain it's not? Can you be certain you understand God's plan in this season? No. But you can be certain to choose His joy and trust Him through it.

If you are in Christ, you have been given the gift of the great freedom to not allow circumstances and feelings to dictate your peace and joy. That doesn't mean that you become emotionless, unaffected by things around you. But it does mean that you don't need to continue to walk heavy and frustrated when God's joy is readily available to you right now. You don't need to feel depressed that you're not where you think you should be. Sister, if God is in control and you're following Him, you can't go off course. It's a matter of deciding whether you'll walk in belief or not. It's your choice—this very day—to put off bitterness and expectation and to put on His joy and His peace.

CHAPTER 8

The Wise Listen to Counsel: Pursuing Victory among the Advisers

Surely you need guidance to wage war, and victory is won through many advisers.
(Prov. 24:6)

When I was seeking my own answers, I read several great books on the topic. Any good presentation requires research, and I wanted to present here the best research that I found among those excellent authors. This doesn't mean that the other authors are infallible or that I've read every great book on the subject. However, I would not have been able to understand these topics as thoroughly as I do today without the many wise counselors who have formulated sound biblical answers on the topic of purity.

This section covers what I would consider to be some of the FAQs on sexual purity. I've asked many of these questions in my own heart, and I've heard others ask them as well. The questions are directly addressed from the Word of God and other authors' reflections. While I've done my best to answer in full honor to His Word, I encourage you to read the Scriptures I reference here and let the Holy Spirit do His own teaching directly with you.

While these aren't listed in any order of importance, I want to begin where we should always begin—with the Word of God.

What Bible references specifically talk about sexual purity?

The entire Bible is profitable for instruction in righteousness (2 Tim. 3:16). This is one of the most important connections in understanding this topic. While there are Scriptures that directly address sexual purity, it's imperative that you don't isolate them from the rest of the Word as I initially tried to do. Without understanding the full picture of the saving power and redemptive nature of Jesus Christ as presented in a full reading of the Bible, these verses out of context may be misunderstood and not fully appreciated for the layers of important meaning that exist well beyond the surface. Yet as you develop your understanding of God's call to purity in your own walk with Him, I encourage you to become familiar with how the topic is handled in each of these references. The passages listed below are the most common ones directly addressing sexual purity:

- Eph. 5:3–5, 11–12, 21–25
- Gal. 5:19–21
- Gen. 1:28; 2:21–25
- Heb. 13:4
- 1 Cor. 5:1; 6:9–20; 7:1–9; 10:8, 13; 13:4–8
- 2 Cor. 7:1; 10:5, 13; 12:21
- Matt. 5:27–30; 15:19–20
- Mark 7:20–23; 10:6–9
- 1 Thess. 4:3–8
- Prov. 5:15–19; 6:32; 28:13
- Eccl. 12:13–14
- Song 7:6–12
- Jude 1:7
- Jer. 17:9–10
- Titus 2:12
- Acts 15:19–20, 29
- Col. 3:5
- Ex. 20:3–4, 14
- Rom. 1:24–27; 13:9–14

- 1 Tim. 1:10
- 2 Tim. 2:22
- 1 John 2:15–16
- 1 Pet. 2:11
- Deut. 22:13–21
- Lev. 18; 20:13
- Ps. 16:11; 19:14; 24:3–5; 51:10
- James 1:14–15
- Rev. 21:8

I'm in a relationship and we've already had sex before marriage. What's the point of stopping now until we're married? Haven't we already blown it?

You're no different than the rest of this world of imperfect people. We are all sinners in need of the Savior. When Jesus died on the cross, He did so to provide everlasting redemption and restoration for our sin. Yet we cannot choose to stay in our sin and attempt to have a close relationship with God at the same time.

In her book *And the Bride Wore White: Seven Secrets to Sexual Purity*, Dannah Gresh presents a great discussion about a divided heart:

> When someone's heart is healthy, the four chambers beat in rhythm. What would happen if half of the heart decided it wasn't feeling much like working with the other half? You might have palpita-

tions, or your heart might skip a beat. It could hurt a lot, or you could barely notice it. It would not be an immediate death sentence, but your body would become weaker and weaker if that half of the heart kept resisting the responsibility to do its job in conjunction with the other half. Eventually, that "divided heart" would ruin the quality of your life and it might one day actually kill you.[5]

There's no way around it. Choosing to stay in our sin is evidence of a divided heart. Would you want to be in a relationship with someone who was only half in it with you?

Think about it another way. Often when people go on a diet, they have a cheat day during the week and allow themselves to eat what they want, assuming that they've been disciplined the other six days. It may sound like a good idea, but most people underestimate the amount of damage that can be done in a single day or, in the case of sexual purity, in just a brief moment.

Sexual sin is the only sin referenced in the Bible that's said to be committed against one's own flesh. The consequence of this sin includes deep and dangerous scars that can taint our thinking, our memories, our health, and our ability to have a healthy relationship

5. Dannah Gresh, *And the Bride Wore White: Seven Secrets to Sexual Purity* (Chicago: Moody Publishers, 2012), 46–47.

with another person. Most importantly, this sin creates distance in our relationship with our Creator. Our sin separates us from God (Isa. 59:2). Yet as we purposely seek to remove ourselves from sin and draw closer to Him, He also draws closer to us (James 4:8).

God doesn't give us passes for cheat days, and He doesn't want our heart divided between Him and something else. He wants us. Every part of us. When we realize that what we're doing is sinful, the Bible tells us that we can't stay in that sin and claim to love God.

Jesus can redeem, heal, restore, and renew your relationship in a way that you can't yet picture or understand if you're blinded by sin. Dabbling in sin even once in a while is a dangerous and purposeful separation from holiness that also separates you from the blessings of obedience. But you don't have to take my word for it. Try it yourself. Stop the sinful behavior now. Refuse to maintain a divided heart. Trust God with all your heart to empower you to proceed in holiness no matter what the past looks like, and see if His blessings don't surpass everything you've dreamed of or imagined (Eph. 3:20).

I'm in my sexual peak. I'm also single. Does God really expect me to continue to wait to find Mr. Right? Isn't this the time I should be enjoying myself the most?

Sisters, hopefully you understand by now that I fully relate to the struggle of celibacy during the sexual peak period—for most women, between the ages of twenty-five and forty-five—as that was the same time I was between marriages and newly single. It was an incredible struggle and one my husband and I could have survived only by the power of the Holy Spirit.

If you happen to find yourself in the midst of this period, you've been called to one of the highest training grounds of your Christian walk. You may think your emotions, desires, or struggles are intense during this period, but the Word promises that they simply will not compare to the glory that is to come (Rom. 8:18).

Greg Speck's book *Sex: It's Worth Waiting For* is one of the most comprehensive Bible-based discussions of this topic that I've ever read. In talking about a guy's sexual peak, he puts it like this:

> Guys ask me, "How come we reach our sexual peak so early when we can't do anything about it?" It is because God wants to develop character in your life. He wants you to be a man with self-control.[6]

Have you ever considered God's perfect plan in this design? Men are called to purity during their peak,

_____

6. Greg Speck, *Sex: It's Worth Waiting For* (Chicago: Moody Publishers, 2007), 21.

typically between the ages of fifteen and twenty-five, a time when most men aren't yet married. In other words, God is calling men to purity at an age when there might not be any holy outlet for that desire. I'm almost certain that most men would consider staying pure during that time an impossible task. By human standards, it is. But God also considers men to be the leaders in their homes and in their families. What better time to take on the most intense training period of their lives than before stepping into this role of headship? If a young man can develop the great fruit of Spirit-led self-control during his most intense fleshly battle, how much better will he be as a husband and father who can lead his wife and children in producing the same fruit?

Tempering is the primary goal of Christian consecration. When a knife maker is ready to harden a knife blade, he heats it until it's glowing red and then plunges it into oil to temper it. If the blade does not go through this process, it will crack the moment it's stressed to function as it was designed to do. A caterpillar goes through a process that mirrors death before it becomes a butterfly. Without tempering—sometimes by extreme circumstances, training, or even what may feel like breaking—all things, from the butterfly to the blade, simply wouldn't be prepared for what they are meant to be.

Women, if the man you're dating is a man of God who has learned the virtue of self-control, what a blessing for you to be in fellowship with someone who has faced this battle already. While we may not understand God's reason for the different periods of sexual interest in a man and woman's lives, we can rest assured that it is designed with purpose. Can you imagine if God had designed it that women and men peaked at the same period of life? It would probably look much like the cities of Corinth or Sodom and Gomorrah. God never wanted a life of debauchery for us.

I also want to debunk the lie that whispers, "If I don't enjoy sex now during this peak time, I won't enjoy it or I may not even want it later." That's ridiculous. You can't put a limit on God's blessings, and we can't, in our limited human minds, understand the value of obedience until we experience it firsthand. Delayed gratification for the purpose of holiness always increases, never decreases, satisfaction.

Step up onto the holy ground you've been called to. It may be shorter in duration than you can foresee, but you won't know until you fully embrace this season and this calling. Fighting to take your place as one set apart is simply that, a fight. But taking on the fight in your own strength is not only unnecessary, but will undoubtedly result in you getting hurt. Step up, heed the call, and let the Master do the fighting for you. "The Lord will fight for you; you need only to be still" (Ex. 14:14).

I'm a Christian, which means I'm free in Christ and am redeemed from the eternal consequence of my sin. If Jesus already paid the price and I'm truly free, then why all these limitations?

Again, Greg Speck has knocked it out of the park with his discussion here. Check it out:

> It's important that we realize there are limitations in all of God's creation. For example, take a cute little sparrow. Isn't it a shame that this bird is limited to sky and land only? Three-fourths of the earth's surface is covered by water. It isn't fair—this sparrow should be able to go underwater.
>
> . . . Or take a big, beautiful rainbow trout. It's not fair that this fish should be limited to the water. There is so much to do and see on land.
>
> . . . Finally take a kitten, a tiny fur ball. Would you say, "It isn't fair that this kitten is limited to the ground—it should have the opportunity to fly?" So we take the kitten to the top of the Sears Tower and throw it off. "You're free! Fly, fly, fly! . . . Wow, little kitty is a now a big mess."
>
> This was not freedom for the sparrow, the trout or the kitten; because their freedom is found within the limitations of what God has created them to be

and to become.

. . . Yes we're free within limitations, and you will discover that these limitations will actually heighten your joy and give you life that is really satisfying.[7]

Don't believe the lie that tells you that you're missing something because you've chosen to align with God's purpose and plan for your life. You'd be as foolish as a kitten trying to fly.

I've already had premarital sex. Does it really matter at this point how many partners I've had? What's the big deal if it's only one more?

Hopefully you understand that this is sin. God's plan was for one man and one woman to enjoy sex within the confines of marriage. That should be enough for you to know that you shouldn't go outside of that plan. But if you are still not convinced, let me give you another perspective on the incredibly dangerous territory you're stepping into.

The gift of sex within marriage isn't just a physical gift. It's a spiritual, mental, and emotional gift as well. Like many other things within His creation, God has purposely designed sex to multitask. It bonds you and

---

7. Speck, *Sex: It's Worth Waiting For*, 37–38.

your spouse into "one flesh" (Gen. 2:24) and creates a oneness that no one should sever. Extensive research shows that chemicals are released during sex that emotionally and mentally connect you to each other. Together in sexual union, you create memories that may be impossible to ever erase from your mind as you explore new territory together. You give yourself, fully exposed, vulnerable, and transparent, in a way like no other. It's a transcendent experience—a high that research also shows, in studies of the brain during sex, exhibits incredible similarity to a brain high on addictive drugs. God has designed sex to be one of the best natural mental, physical, emotional, and spiritual highs possible. You can't claim to have safe sex because you use a condom, as you're only addressing one aspect of sex, the physical part. You can't protect yourself from the mental, emotional, spiritual, and other physical responses your body will naturally experience in sex. You can't protect yourself from it, because you weren't supposed to.

And sisters, your husband can't protect himself either. Consider this. Would you want your husband shared among multiple people before he's given in marriage to you? If you've had a difficult time forgetting past lovers, don't you think he will as well? Is there any part of you that can stomach him thinking about a past lover while he makes love to you? Unholy sexual memories are so dangerous because they can be triggered within holy sex. Of course, you can (and should) rebuke and take the thoughts captive—but do you really want your husband preoccupied with this battle while he should be enjoying and pleasing you? Do *you* want to endure this battle?

God didn't intend for sex to be shared territory. He didn't want Eve to experience the fruit that would give her the knowledge of the unholy, because He knew neither she nor Adam would ever be the same. If you truly consider that premarital sex not only takes something sacred from your future husband but also that you're creating a shared space, even in memory, for that which is supposed to be for only him and you, you'll realize that this temporary moment of release is just not worth the years (and I do mean years) of painful consequences. Sharing your body with others now is the same as giving them a key to the house that you and your husband will share together someday.

Rebuke the lie that says you might be missing out by saying no to anyone who isn't your spouse. You are securing the locks of sacredness on your marital home.

Also reject the lie that tells you a little more isn't such a big deal. We've all heard that voice, especially with our favorite sin. It's the same lie you hear from drug dealers, gamblers, and anyone with a stronghold of sin, and it originates from the father of lies (John 8:44). A little sin is not okay in God's eyes. If it's okay with you, then it's evidence of a divided heart. How do you deal with a divided heart? Discern truth by believing and accepting only God's Word as truth. Consider this statement from Pastor Deon O. Thomas in his book *21 Days to Sexual Purity: A Biblical Devotional for Overcoming Sexual Temptations*: "Sexual immoral desires arise from within the heart (Matt. 15:19). It is the heart that needs to be changed. Our hearts are changed as we believe the word of God."[8]

If you're still not convinced, check out the many research studies that prove that monogamous, married couples are generally more satisfied with their relationships and their sex life. They're less prone to depression and even some diseases. Several studies found a direct link to higher sexual satisfaction, including more orgasms among "religious" couples or couples who regularly go to church. For more information and a simple explanation of some of this research, check out Jonathan McKee's book *Sex Matters*.

What if it's not in God's plan for me to get married? Am I really supposed to refrain from sex for my entire life?

---

8. Deon O. Thomas, *21 Days to Sexual Purity: A Biblical Devotional for Overcoming Sexual Temptations* (self-pub. CreateSpace, 2014), 29.

Soon after I got saved, I got a card from someone at church quoting Psalm 20:4, which says, "May He [God] give you the desire of your heart and make all your plans succeed."

Well, I thought, this was just great. I wanted an awesome husband, and I had plans to have great sex. I was glad someone else was praying this for me too!

Then I learned that's not quite the correct application of that verse. This Scripture is actually a prayer that God will download into your heart that which He wants you to desire. He puts us on a path to fulfill those desires when we submit to Him. He doesn't review your wish list and manifest your dream car, lover, job, and house, as if He were some genie. He knows us better than we know ourselves, and He knows what will give us the greatest fulfillment. Psalm 20:4 reveals the profound truth that He desires that you willingly ask Him to change your desires to align with His good plan for you. I have seen God change my heart on subjects I believed I was absolutely set on. I now look back in amazement and can't even remember how I rationalized thinking the way I did at the time. Time and time again, God has moved my heart in ways that I didn't ask for and have only benefited from.

So first, my sister, you must believe that His plan is good—no matter what. I'm not telling you that you have to get excited or even happy about the idea of a lifetime of celibacy, although there are some great benefits to singleness and celibacy. I'm only encouraging you to believe that your Savior's plan was a good one from start to finish, including whatever He has planned for you. That's your first step. Get your focus off yourself and onto Him.

Your second step is to seek first the kingdom. In Matthew 6:33 (NKJV), the Bible says, "Seek first the kingdom of God and His righteousness, and all these things shall be added to you." Sister, you will be provided for. This is God's ultimate promise to you. I have no idea what God's specific plan is for you, but I'm absolutely certain that if you're His, it's an amazing, beautiful plan that would blow your mind if you could get a glimpse of it.

Sounds likes it's easier said than done, especially coming from a married woman, right? I promise that the grass is only greener on His side. Married or single, great sex or no sex, it honestly doesn't make that much of a difference if He's not in it with you. Remember, I've done marriage and sex with and without Him. There's no comparison. If you hope for God to bless you with the ministry of a marriage (and it is a ministry), get prepared beginning now by simply stepping over to His side and aligning your heart with His.

Now is the time to share the deepest parts of yourself with Him. Don't be afraid to ask for what you desire.

But the more important thing is to ask Him, as Psalm 20:4 suggests, to give you that which He wants you to desire. Do you understand that by asking that, you are essentially asking God to prepare your heart for the excitement around the corner? Aligning your heart to His in this way doesn't leave you hanging, not knowing if you will receive what you're desiring. Aligning your heart with His ensures that He will create the desire, excitement, and anticipation in you for that which He has already prepared.

Sister, you truly can enjoy a fulfilled heart, no matter what your circumstance, as long as you are His (Ps. 23:1). Remember that He was the One who created your needs in the first place. Your heart and your life and all your other needs will be taken care of because He's the perfect One to do it.

The critical question is, do you believe that? My prayer for you is that your answer is a resounding yes.

Many times, women are the ones avoiding sex and men are the ones pursuing it. Not me. I have a higher sex drive than even most men I know. How do I reconcile this desire and passion within me when it doesn't seem to fit the norm?

Girl, let me just get right in front of the mirror for this discussion. I've had it with myself and my God many times. I'm here to finally give you some cause for celebration and some good news. Tim Alan Gardner sums it up in his wonderful book *Sacred Sex: A Spiritual Celebration of Oneness in Marriage*: "The desire to be loved and needed by another human being, the hunger to know that our life matters to someone else, is a God-given need."[9]

Your desire—assuming that it's rooted in holiness—is good and God-given. God has gifted you with a desire to experience His gift. If that desire is that strong, you can rest assured that His provision will meet your need as well. But there are a few things to consider to ensure you're in a holy place with it.

First, the Bible tells us to examine ourselves carefully to properly view our own sin (Matt. 7:1–5). Is your need for sex rooted in a need for affirmation, love, or other reassurance? Those areas must first be filled by the love of Christ before you can enjoy holy sex properly. Consider what Gardner says:

> We must first find our significance in God. That means we don't base our significance on our good looks, our mate's beautiful body, or a successful sex life. To find genuine significance, we must first

9. Tim Alan Gardner, *Sacred Sex: A Spiritual Celebration of Oneness in Marriage* (Colorado Springs: WaterBrook Press, 2002), 175.

have our shame removed by the cross of Christ. We must first stand naked and unashamed before God. Only then will we begin to find the significance that lasts.[10]

Second, you don't need to compare yourself to anyone else. Not only is this ungodly, but it's ridiculous. We can't possibly begin to know what truly goes on within the hearts and homes of other people, even those closest to us. Your best friend may be avoiding sex with her husband for all sorts of unholy reasons and claiming it as a low sex drive. Or you may know someone who is addicted to sex because it has become an idol mimicking love in her life, so she claims to have a high sex drive. These intimate, soul-level things simply can't be known about others through observation.

Third, contrary to popular belief, men—at least men of God—aren't all about sex for sex. Their sex drive isn't limited to the physical aspect. Gardner states, "Many women fail to understand how deeply sex can be connected to emotional oneness for their husbands."[11] Comparing your sex drive even to a man's sex drive is not an appropriate comparison either, because there are too many elements affecting him other than the physical.

Gardner continues:

---

10. Gardner, *Sacred Sex,* 78.
11. Gardner, *Sacred Sex,* 101.

Many men do a very poor job articulating the
incredibly intense and immense sensations that
are occurring within them far beyond what is
happening on the physiological level. To many
men, being one sexually is the place where they
feel most one—most naked and unashamed—with
their mates. However, if they are unable to fully
communicate that to their wives, their desire for
sex can come across as just that: a desire for sex.[12]

Even if your sex drive doesn't match those of other
men you've been with in the past or of your husband
currently, there's more going on than meets the eye.
And God can change anything He needs to change to
ensure proper oneness between you and your spouse in
due time.

Finally, God doesn't make mistakes. He didn't make
a mistake giving you a desire for sex—even if you're not
currently in a marriage to be able to enjoy it. I'm not
saying it's easy, but you must understand that God has
not made a mistake with you. When my husband and
I finally got together, he revealed that he had prayed
to God for some very specific things in a woman and
that I was the manifestation of those answered prayers.
The things he specifically prayed for were things that I

---

12. Gardner, *Sacred Sex*, 101.

wrestled with, often not appreciating those things about myself and wondering if God had made a mistake! God used me to answer the prayers of my beloved. Is there anything better than being used for that purpose? What if I told you today that even your flaws are things that God has planned for His purposes and His good plan, custom-created for you.

Passionate, sex-loving sister, calm down and stop beating yourself up or comparing yourself to anyone else. It took me a while to realize that God had a good plan for what I was previously wrestling with—and it all came together when I met my husband and recognized that God had been preparing me in a way that would satisfy my husband specifically. Hallelujah! If God has given you a need, it's His job to fill it.

My boyfriend and I fool around a little, but we stop before either has an orgasm and we don't have sex. That's okay, right?

The awesome purpose of foreplay is that it's meant to lead somewhere. It's the physical GPS to God's great gift to married couples. If you think of it more like a GPS (rather than a bag of potato chips where you think you can stop at just one), you'll understand that there's no point for either of you to get in the car, activate the

GPS, and then sit there and watch it without actually getting to the destination.

Going back to the bag of potato chips theory—chips are bad for your health. Sex (with your spouse) is not. There are hundreds of articles published on the health and relationship benefits of sex. (Read them with a guarded heart, understanding that the benefits and blessings only truly come to married couples.) You should not want to rob you or your husband of any part of the phenomenal gift that is coming your way on your wedding night by previewing it. Remember when you were a kid and sneaked downstairs to see what had been left under the Christmas tree for you before your parents were awake? It's a little bit like that. We get a preview but still have to wait, and then the moment of revelation has changed a bit. It's less heightened because the rush isn't there in the way it would have been without the preview.

Yet another example. Have you ever gone to a movie and watched a trailer for a comedy only to find out when the movie came out that the preview already showed you the funniest part? So frustrating! When that part in the movie was shown, it was still enjoyable, but it certainly didn't impact you the way it could have if you hadn't seen that funny part already in the preview. Looking back, you almost wished you hadn't seen the preview at all. They showed you the best in the preview, and your experience of watching the entire movie was diminished as a result. I'm not saying that you can't fully experience pleasure in sex if you've already had a good preview of it, but I am saying that you can't experience the full holiness of the revelation as God planned it to be.

And wives-to-be, like I mentioned earlier, would you really want your husband giving away a preview to someone else? Of course not, because other women are not going to be his wife! But currently you aren't either. If you're not his wife and you're engaging with him sexually (even without intercourse or orgasm), you are taking what is not yours. It's not yours to take, and it's not even his to give, since as believers our bodies no longer belong to us (1 Cor. 6:19). God will give the gift of each other's bodies to you both once you take your covenant vow to Him.

Think about it another way. Can you imagine how it will enhance your wedding night if the list of firsts you both experience as a couple is longer than just the obvious one of intercourse? Can you imagine the incredible pleasure and rush of discovering one another in every way for the very first time with no boundaries, no limitations, no hiding, and no mixing of shame with pleasure? This, my sisters, is pleasure in its purest form in this earthly life.

I want to be clear that I'm not saying that kissing, holding hands, etc. in the premarital stages is wrong, but it's the level of intensity and the intent that can cause problems. It's the address plugged into the GPS—the final destination—that you need to be concerned with. What's a safe address? Jonathan McKee says it well in his book *The Guy's Guide to God, Girls, and the Phone in Your Pocket*: "Don't do anything with your girlfriend you wouldn't do in front of your grandmother."[13] Great line. Play that all out in your mind the next time you're making out. Imagine that one of your grandparents is "in the car" with you and watching you. The safe GPS address for foreplay? Grandma's house.

Here's yet another angle. Engaging in intense foreplay without experiencing the glorious reality of God-blessed sex is no more satisfying than living in a fantasy. In her book *The Fantasy Fallacy: Exposing the Deeper Meaning behind Sexual Thoughts*, Shannon Ethridge explains the implications and effects of sexual fantasy. This book is especially applicable to a female whose mind may be more naturally inclined toward fantasy and desire. Shannon specifically wrote this book in response to the insanity of the *Fifty Shades of Grey* phenomenon. She does a fine job of showing how empty and destructive unholy fantasy becomes in our lives and how rewarding it is to pursue the reality of what God intended and not the fantasy:

---

13. Jonathan McKee, *The Guy's Guide to God, Girls, and the Phone in Your Pocket* (Uhrichsville, OH: Shiloh Run Press, 2014), quoted in *Sex Matters* (Bloomington, MN: Bethany House, 2015), 52.

As we lose ourselves, not in fantasy, but in the reality of sharing our innermost selves with God and with each other, we gain the deepest sense of satisfaction humanly possible. We experience what it means to be truly one flesh with both the Creator and His creation.[14]

Do you realize that Shannon just said that our one-flesh experience extends into both the physical and supernatural realms simultaneously? The reality of holy sex leads to the fantastic experience of supernatural (out of this world) connection that we actually can't even fathom or create in our own experience. Fantasy can't touch reality. Awesome.

In case you're still not convinced, what if I told you that what you're doing in your foreplay may have some seriously negative implications on your wedding night? Wait, what? How so? By repeatedly engaging in intense foreplay and stopping before it reaches intercourse or orgasm, you are essentially creating muscle memory to train your body to not reach orgasm—or at least not to reach it with your future spouse. (Not sure muscle memory is real? Check it out as a training method for professional sports players. I used to be a certified personal trainer and can attest to its incredible success

---

14. Shannon Ethridge, *The Fantasy Fallacy,* 122.

in clients.) Having counseled and talked with many couples about premarital sex and this issue specifically, Greg Speck discusses how this strategy can wreck your honeymoon:

> Premarital sex can cause sexual dysfunctions after you are married. Let's suppose that as a woman you believed strongly that you shouldn't climax with anyone until after you were married. However, you were involved sexually. You just made sure that you stopped before climaxing . . . or maybe you would do everything except have intercourse.
>
> Now you get married, and you're on your honeymoon. You begin to move toward intercourse and climax that first night and then all of a sudden, your body turns off. Why? Because you've programmed it to do just that. You become frustrated; he becomes frustrated, and now you have a problem that didn't have to be if you had waited.
>
> People usually suffer through this type of situation for a while, hoping it will clear up on its own. However, the stress and tensions build, making it even harder to respond.[15]

I believe wholeheartedly that God wants us to enjoy the fulfillment of His good plans for us. If we are seeking

---

15. Speck, *Sex: It's Worth the Wait*, 70.

that within the gift of marital sex, then we should press on in our training in pursuit of victory at the main event. If you truly believe sex is meant to be so great (and it is), can you really justify risking it and impacting it so dramatically by moments of half-pleasure in the present?

I've been divorced and am hesitant to remarry, but I also realize it's the only way that God will bless me in a sexual relationship. I'm not a kid anymore. I've lived life, and I don't plan on dating just to date. How long should I wait to get remarried?

I realize I may be biased because I appreciate Greg Speck's book so much, but it was only after I wrote much of my book that I realized he had given similar advice to this question with the same Scripture referenced earlier regarding the burn (1 Cor. 7:9). Greg states that couples simply don't need to wait so long to get married if, as Paul says, they are more likely to burn with passion if they don't.

The ultimate answer is that you should get married as soon as God directs you both to do so. While I believe it's generally good advice to at least go through every season together (a year or more) prior to marriage, there's no set timetable. But God needs to move both of your hearts, not just one. One of the main aspects of marriage, as we've discussed, is for God to make you one with your husband. He won't begin that without first aligning your hearts. If one of you has no desire to get married, this isn't the relationship to continue in.

I once had a guy give me a ring on the second date. Really. And I was foolish enough to take it. Discretion, reflection, and revelation often take time, especially when a fellow human is doing their best to show you only their best. You've got to see some ugly before you say yes; otherwise, you're only saying yes to the lovely.

When Geoff and I married after about a year of a committed courting relationship, some people felt like it was too soon. Having both been previously divorced and both of us having children from those marriages, we intended to be very cautious and well prepared for such a decision. But God had done the preparation in us that we needed for the call when it came. When we both separately heard the call to marry one another, we knew in His eyes that we were ready, no matter what the rest of the world thought.

Did we have it all together? Absolutely not. In fact, when we decided to get married, we still had no concrete plan to rectify the three-hour distance between us. It wasn't an easy issue to ignore, either; there were multiple families, schools, jobs, and two separate established homes to account for and somehow collaborate. To our onlookers, there were just too many things that we hadn't properly settled before the decision to get married. But we were both absolutely certain of the call and proceeded in faith toward it anyway. And in God's good and perfect timing, we married. Two weeks before the wedding, God revealed and confirmed the solution of my relocation to Virginia.

His timing, His plan, His way. It's the only way to go. When He calls you both, make sure it's really Him speaking. Check what you're hearing against the Word. If the call and the Word align, then proceed prayerfully.

So if my boyfriend and I refrain from sexual foreplay prior to marriage, how will we know if we're actually compatible in this area? Isn't this a key part of marriage to find out about ahead of time? I've heard it's important to take a "test drive."

Before getting saved, I was the one in my circle of friends who was the biggest supporter of the "test drive." I confidently touted that this was the only way to go. And that's exactly what I did. Going my own way (in this and other areas), instead of God's, led me to divorce. I was foolish and prideful, at best.

Am I saying that anyone who has had sex prior to marriage and then gets married will get divorced? Of course not. The beauty of God's grace is that when you turn to seek Him with your whole heart, His redemptive powers are magnificently magnified. But I can only write this because I have seen and experienced both sides. The test drive is a false gauge and gives unreliable information.

First and most obviously, the whole notion of the test drive to determine compatibility is faulty because God already designed the male and female bodies to be perfectly compatible. The mechanics have already been settled.

If there are other emotional or physical conditions that could interfere in a healthy sex life, then these issues should be discussed openly prior to marriage. But even with preexisting conditions or past difficulties, God can and does actively redeem and provide for His children as they seek Him. So even in a more extreme case, if two people are willing to proceed to marriage with the goal of glorifying Him, then He will also provide well for them. I'm not saying that all your problems will go away, but I am saying that the only true problem is not bringing God into it. Really, what this whole issue lends itself to is a matter of your level of trust with the Savior.

If we consider God's design and that the root of this issue stems from pride, we'll see it in a whole different light. If you truly believe that God knows best, you will trust His plan to be good and not insist on a test drive.

Is there any other way to explore sexual compatibility prior to marriage? Possibly, but I want to caution you that this is controversial, so I also ask you to proceed in prayer and guard your heart before you consider what I'm about to say.

There's nothing wrong with talking about sex with your future spouse to discuss likes, dislikes, expectations, and interests. I think this is valuable and healthy information as long as you both can keep your hearts and bodies guarded well during the conversation. Now comes the obvious question: Is that realistic? Can we discuss sex in depth—with the one we are trying desperately not to have it with—without temptation growing and growing? That's a valid question, and I'll explain two sides of this because I don't want to stand entirely on my own understanding here.

Dannah Gresh, author of *And the Bride Wore White: Seven Secrets to Sexual Purity*, says this is a no-go. She says that not only should girls refrain from discussing sex, physical contact, and physical desires with a boyfriend, but it's a risk to our purity as it normalizes sexual familiarity and makes desires even more difficult to control.[16] I believe this is solid advice that's very important with a younger audience such as Dannah's, as it likely includes guys in their sexual peak who are especially tempted. Sexual conversation may be a stumbling block not only for the one speaking it, but also for the one hearing it,

---

16. Dannah Gresh, *And the Bride Wore White*, 98–99.

and could lead both into temptation. The Bible says we're to flee from sexual immorality (1 Cor. 6:18).

On the other hand, when I began dating again after my first marriage, I was interacting with men who were beyond their "peak" years. Some of the men I met who were beyond this stage of their life were not as vulnerable; self-control wasn't a fruit of the Spirit that was new to them. This wasn't, of course, the case with everyone, but I did meet men with whom I could have mature and intelligent discussions around even difficult topics without blurring holy lines. I do believe that a reasonable and informative discussion of sex is possible between mature men and women who are walking out purity in action and with great discernment.

My husband and I had discussions about sex prior to marriage. In fact, we spoke about it in detail—not with the intent to tempt one another—but rather to understand how previous experiences would impact the future of our relationship. We both found these discussions to be informative and important. Our experience may not translate in application to all other Christian couples, though, especially those who have not been previously married.

Talking about sex with Geoff before marriage was no different from some of the conversations I would have (and sometimes still do have) with my closest girlfriends, however. We often laugh and share insight, and sometimes it's even a great place for organic discipleship to occur. Geoff and I learned a lot about each other and our past in those conversations, and I have never regretted or had any personal conviction about those conversations. Could we have been playing with fire? I believe someone could reasonably argue that. Yet if feelings or desires are not driving actions, if hearts are seeking God, and if neither is succumbing to temptation because of conversations like this, then I don't think you can claim they're sinful in themselves.

I believe this is one of those areas that the Bible could be referring to when it says, "'I have the right to do anything,' you say—but not everything is beneficial. 'I have the right to do anything'—but not everything is constructive" (1 Cor. 10:23).

We need to be extremely careful not to cause another, especially a beloved partner, to stumble (1 Cor. 8:13). So please proceed with caution and consider Dannah's viewpoint seriously, as hers is the more conservative (and likely safer) route.

God is trustworthy to provide you with the partner you need—not necessarily checking all the boxes of what you want—but He will indeed give you what you need if you're seeking first the kingdom and trusting Him wholeheartedly. You don't need to have any conversations about sex with your future spouse before marriage as some sort of insurance policy for a great sex life.

The test drive, however, is absolutely off limits. Your body, heart, and soul are blatantly exposed to unholiness when you do. But can you talk about sex with your boyfriend before you are married? Yes, if your GPS is set for Grandma's house, hearts are guarded, and intentions are pure. Should there be limits? Absolutely—because so much is a stake.

> Above all else, guard your heart, for everything you
> do flows from it.
> (Prov. 4:23)

I've heard people refer to sex as "sacred," but that seems a little extreme. Even if we remain perfectly "pure" until marriage, aren't we still both sinners? Is it still sacred if we've been sexually active before marriage?

From the beginning, God has allowed and invited man to partake in the sacred. In fact, community within the sacred is the very essence of God within the Trinity. God has made man in His image and likeness (Gen. 1:27). God was in blissful communion with Adam and Eve, and they cared for His sacred creation in the Garden. Once man came to know sin, God laid out the steps for him to participate in the rituals to attempt to cleanse himself and participate in the sacred communion once more with God (before Jesus's incarnation).

When Jesus was resurrected, God allowed for the ultimate communion between man and God by having the Holy Spirit come to live inside of His people. While we aren't sacred because of our own righteousness (and are only made righteous by Jesus's blood), God regularly allows for His people to participate in that which is sacred. The joining of one flesh is indeed just that to God, as there is no other act on earth that mimics the sacredness of holy relationship to that degree.

The topic of the sacredness of sex is actually my favorite part of the topic because it's one that I had no understanding of until I read Gardner's book. I highly recommend it for anyone seeking to understand sex from God's perspective. Reflecting on this holy image created within godly sex, Gardner states that it is within the "reunion and rejoining of the male and female—that the fullness of God's image finds its highest expression,"[17] and I would add the words *that we experience among one another.*

In other words, I believe Jesus to be the fullness and greatest expression of God's image—and holy sex to be the fullness of unity that man can experience here on earth within the threefold cord (Eccl. 4:12) of husband, wife, and God. The sacredness of sex is not just the physical uniting of two people. It's the hearts

---

17. Gardner, *Sacred Sex*, 38.

that are seeking God (even more than physical union) and the Holy Spirit providing the supernatural bonding and holy ecstasy that occur as a result. The sacredness of holy sex has everything to do with God's presence within it—and not just the legality of man and woman sharing a name or a bed. It was God's good design to be at the very center of sex, as Tim Gardner confirms all throughout his book that we simply can't "remove sex from the realm of the holy."

Some Christians believe that the primary purpose of sex is procreation, quoting from God's command in Genesis 9:7 (NKJV) to "be fruitful and multiply." There's no arguing that this was a command and certainly a major purpose of sex, but God's full purpose for sex wasn't summed up with this statement. I'm once again in agreement with Tim Gardner, who instead sees the sacredness of holy unification as the greater purpose of sex:

> If you ask the average person in the pew to identify the primary purpose of sex (and if you manage to avoid getting hit with a hymnal), he or she will most likely say either procreation or recreation. Of course, both are rich blessings of sex. But the essence of sexual intimacy can never be enjoyed, nor can true and lasting sexual fulfillment occur, until a wife and a husband grasp the truth that the number-one purpose of sex is neither procreation

nor recreation, but *unification*. And I don't mean just the unification that is inherent in physical oneness, but also the relational unity that is celebrated, created, and re-created throughout a couple's married life. This unification is the celebration of the soul-deep bond that is present when a couple knows and experiences the certainty that they are together, permanently, for a divine purpose. They know their expression of love is meant to represent the loving relationship of Jesus and His church. They know that their life together has meaning that is far greater than simply sharing a house or bearing children. . . . In other words, the "Big O" of sex is not orgasm; it's oneness.[18]

To add a richer element to this discussion, I want to highlight an interesting and beautiful revelation Dannah Gresh provides. Dannah points out that like the other sacred covenants, holy sex is also a blood covenant. Consider God's design with the female body:

In Bible times, a bride and groom were presented with white linens for their wedding night. They were expected to sleep on them, and the bride was expected to bleed on them as proof of her virginity. You see, God created you and me with a protective

---

18. Gardner, *Sacred Sex*, 48–49.

> membrane, the hymen, which in most cases is broken the first time that we have intercourse. When it breaks, a woman's blood spills over her husband. Your sexual union is a blood covenant between you, your husband, and God.[19]

Amen and amen. What a beautiful design in God's creation to represent His intention for holy sex. So if your hymen has already been broken and it wasn't within the holy union of matrimony, does this negate the blood covenant between you and your husband? Thankfully, no. Jesus's blood fulfilled that covenant too. Just understand that His intention was for you to remain in holiness so you could enjoy the fullness of His purpose and grand design of sex as being sacred. It is His design and His presence among husband and wife that makes sex holy. And man, even at his worst, can't change the essence or purpose of God's perfect design.

THE BOTTOM LINE

Don't go it alone, sister. I hope these other "wise counselors" have helped you (as they helped me) seek out the true depth of trusting God and His promises with His creation and His good gifts. This is how we wage the war to victory.

---

19. Dannah Gresh, *And the Bride Wore White*, 129.

CHAPTER 9

Real Submission: As a Single Woman, as a Girlfriend, as a Wife

> In your relationships with one another, have the same mindset as Christ Jesus: Who, being in very nature God, did not consider equality with God something to be used to His own advantage; rather, He made Himself nothing by taking the very nature of a servant, being made in human likeness.
> (Phil. 2:5–7)

Throughout this book I've emphasized that submission is necessary to fully enjoy God's blessings and is a requirement for any holy pursuit. This is absolutely true in pursuing the blessings of sexual purity. If we believe God's way is better, we must walk out that trust in the form of submission. Submission itself is such a powerful response because it demonstrates our trust even in the face of the most intense desires. It is not something we can pull off consistently just by going through the motions. Outward submission without inward alignment will eventually lead to rebellion. When our heart is divided, entrapped by sin or overwhelming emotion, submission can seem like a great task. Yet when our heart is right—rested and trusting in God—our submission will be a voluntary act of our will, reflecting the worthiness of Christ and His perfect example of submission. Aside from aspects just relating to our sexual conduct (or lack thereof), I want to expand the discussion here to look at the different levels of submission within the various stages you may be facing. Some of these have been hard lessons for me to learn.

SUBMISSION IS ALWAYS A CHOICE

To display the heart of the matter, I'd like to share a story that took place two years into my second marriage. It was an average school night, with everyone at home and kids acting crazy. But this average school night was on the end of a five-day span with all my children being home and my husband and me dealing with the constant challenges of a newly blended family with three constantly energetic, aggressive, and competitive boys.

I don't want to sound like I am not grateful for our children being home, but this season had been very hard.

The water in the tub had entirely drained, yet there I remained, sitting in what I can only describe as deep sorrow and darkness, as though someone had died. I wanted to raise my hands in praise to the music I had put on, but I couldn't find the strength to do much of anything but cry deeply. No one knew. My husband was downstairs cleaning the kitchen, and my kids were asleep, or at least pretending to be. I'm pretty certain they all would have been completely caught off guard and shocked by my deep sadness that they would think came out of nowhere.

The truth is, as the only female in the household, most of the time my emotions are not on their radar. I am learning to keep my personal desires and my emotions in the background. Catching moments alone, praying, and sometimes crying to Jesus has become the way of guarding my heart and remaining in submission. I knew I would need the strength to get up to walk in submission again a few moments later. I knew I would need the strength to raise my hands once more in praise. I knew I would need the strength to even get out of the empty tub, where only my tears still drained.

Concentrating my efforts to less than an hour to avoid drawing unnecessary attention to my temporary solitude, I told the Holy Spirit I was entirely letting Him take me over and drive. I had nothing more to give. I couldn't even fake joy (not that true joy can be faked, by the way). The only thing I could do was walk.

With a semi-cheerful heart, I rejoined my husband in the kitchen to finish helping. After that, we watched about an hour of TV and then went to bed. I purposely made a choice to dismiss "Joanna" as much as I could. It was when my husband unexpectedly embraced me to tell me how much he loved me that I felt some of myself come back in.

I would love to tell you that my struggling heart was healed from his words, but hearts don't heal from people. My heart, instead, in its rebellious state, answered inside (silently from the background), *It's not me that you love.*

Immediately a response audible only to my heart sounded: "It's Me."

It almost took my breath away. It was the Holy Spirit telling me that what Geoff saw was what he loved. And in that moment, having dismissed myself as much as I could figure out how to do, Geoff was able to see that which is the only pure part of me—the Holy Spirit within me. It was in this moment that I was reminded that my ultimate call in my role as wife is to show him Jesus. And I simply cannot do that when I'm not in submission. In that moment Geoff was telling Jesus that he loved Him, and as a Christian wife there is nothing more important that I do than help reinforce and reflect that relationship between them.

There is nothing more important I can do. This is the depth, the blessing, and the importance of the call to submission.

THE STARTING POINT

Where, though, do we as women begin the process of submission, especially when we have been taught that independence is key and that reliance on men is foolish and weak? First, we need to accept the Bible as the standard of truth and begin conforming our lives to it. If you don't know where to start, please consult the book *CROWN: 30 Wife-Changing Lessons*, written by my dear friend Nancy Kaser. It is a comprehensive teaching on wife-discipleship that surpasses almost all other books I've read dedicated to the topic. I had the pleasure of being one of her editors, but even while I was editing the book, it was discipling me and changing my marriage. So I know from personal experience that it will be a great help—even if you are not yet married.

Let's begin by talking about what for me might have been the greatest challenge of submission, how this translates through the various stages of singleness, togetherness, and oneness, and then, ultimately, the incredible benefits of submission.

THE CHALLENGE OF SUBMISSION

I believe the greatest challenge of submission is loneliness. If you placed the words *celibacy* and *submission* side by side and asked a group of people which word they would associate more with loneliness, I believe most would choose *celibacy*. As we discussed earlier, there is a misconception about celibacy and loneliness going hand in hand.

Ironically, it's actually the opposite, according to Scripture. With celibacy, you're focused entirely on your Savior without distraction. Along with God, you're preparing to be in the most intimate relationship possible with another human being when He blesses that timing. During this time, you have unhindered potential to inspire, encourage, and make disciples because you aren't splitting your time with your duties as a wife. For most, celibacy isn't a lifelong condition, but a temporary one. While the lack of a physical relationship can create a sense of loneliness for some people (myself included), I've learned that when you're truly focused on God and serving others, there really isn't much room for loneliness. It doesn't have control when you let God have control.

Submission, however, is a lifelong commitment, not a temporary one. Submission is a matter of the heart and will test your humility at every turn. (Lisa Chan gives a great discussion of this with her husband, Francis

Chan, in their book *You and Me Forever: Marriage in Light of Eternity*.) Submission comes with requirements despite marital status, and arguably even more so within a marriage relationship. Submission requires that you consider the other person better than yourself and their needs more important than yours. It further requires that your sense of control needs to die and that you willingly let God handle the result, no matter how it looks to you.

By the way, all this should be done with a cheerful attitude, without a martyr-like demeanor or display, and must include your enemies, not just your loved ones. Submission is very much like silent suffering hidden behind a covering of sincere gratitude and joy. It is sacrifice made entirely out of love, void of self and void of the appearance of suffering during it.

As *CROWN* author Nancy Kaser says, "Thank God submission doesn't require our feelings." Is there anyone else who will recognize just how hard it is on the inside for you to submit to your horrible boss who has just cheated another unsuspecting client, conveniently screwed up your paycheck, and guilted you into working the last four weekends? Is there anyone else on earth who will feel so incredibly betrayed when your child, whom you've lovingly raised, blessed, and given everything for, suddenly goes prodigal and steals from you and lies about it? Is there anyone else on earth who would feel so personally devastated when you discover your spouse's hidden long-term affair?

There is no other person (besides Jesus) who can relate to the pain that you face in the choice of submission in these circumstances. Your comfort will be in knowing that the Holy Spirit inside you will (and has already) empowered you to handle the struggle you face as you submit as Christ did. You can trust Him to reconcile it and even work it for your good.

So while we've talked about the deep and challenging commitment of celibacy, I ask you to take a different perspective, to consider what you will have to do for the rest of your life as a follower of Christ who is called to holy submission. Is there anything harder than celibacy? Yes. Submission.

Is there anything harder than submission? No. Not in this life. In fact, we needed God to intercede on our behalf because only He could accomplish the submission required to save us from ourselves. In the darkest moment in history, His ultimate submission resulted in His ultimate isolation. For Jesus to submit completely to being the perfect sacrifice, He had to be temporarily isolated from the Father and the Holy Spirit. Think about that. The ultimate submission required Jesus to be separated from God the Father because He "who had no sin" had to "be sin for us" (2 Cor. 5:21). This is because God the Father can't be in the presence of sin.

Jesus also made it known that the Holy Spirit couldn't come to indwell believers until Jesus died and ascended to heaven (John 16:7). So in submission, Jesus became isolated from heaven, the Holy Spirit, and God the Father in order to be a perfect sacrifice on our behalf.

Do you realize when we talk about being isolated and lonely that Jesus literally did what we can't do for ourselves in separating from the Father? The Bible says that God the Father will never leave nor forsake us and nothing can separate us from His love (Deut. 31:8; Rom. 8:38–39). While the Father's love for Jesus didn't cease, consider what Jesus said during His darkest moment on earth: "My God, my God, why have you forsaken me?" (Matt. 27:46). No child of God will ever have to utter these words because Jesus chose to suffer this for us. I'm not sure which was more heartbreaking for Jesus—being crucified by those whom He created while pleading to His Father for their forgiveness or enduring the darkness of separation from His Father.

Is submission lonelier than celibacy? I'd say so.

By the way, Jesus never complained about celibacy. Not once. But the Scripture above confirms the incomprehensible pain and isolation He felt at the height of submission when He cried out those words.

So looking at the man across the table or living room from you, is it possible you could do a better job of showing God some love by submitting a little more to this man? Or if that man isn't present yet, could you turn your eyes to the One who is and deepen your submission to Him?

With all this talk of loneliness and pain, if you're not convinced that submission is worthwhile, I understand. It took me a while to understand it also. Keep reading; we'll be covering that shortly.

Ultimately, this is between you and God. If you're a believer, the Holy Spirit will not only empower you, but He will guide you through discernment and Scripture on how to lay yourself down for others (including your boyfriend or husband) in the way that pleases the Lord. If you're a single woman (no husband or even a boyfriend), you have an incredible platform ahead of you as a training ground. Let's see what submission looks like in the phases of singleness, togetherness, and oneness, and then we'll talk about the ultimate benefits of submission.

SUBMISSION IN SINGLENESS

I hadn't practiced biblical submission at all when I was married the first time. Once I got saved and when I was newly single between marriages, I sought to learn what biblical submission looked like. When I did start dating, I attempted to apply some of what I was learning into practice as a girlfriend. There are some ways in which practicing submission as a girlfriend is appropriate and some ways in which it isn't. It's appropriate, for instance, to let the man lead in terms of the pace of your relationship and plans for the future. (Leading is not dictating.) It's not appropriate to give him access to your bank account before marriage or to live together before marriage. When a husband and wife are willing to make the commitment to become one flesh, the less important issue of their possessions follows, not the other way around. But we'll talk more about being a girlfriend in the next section because it's the next stage.

You've likely heard the sayings "You don't find the right one; you become the right one," or "You have to work on you before you can work on a relationship." There is some wisdom in these statements as long as you understand them from a biblical perspective. The key to submission in singleness is not to act like you're single, but rather to act like the bride of Christ that you are. You're to work on becoming a disciple of Christ and do all you can to pursue sanctification by submitting to the Holy Spirit in you. This is the work you do while keeping in mind for Whom you are doing it.

Without meaning to sound cliché, there is great value in acting as if Jesus is your husband. Note that I didn't say, "Jesus is your boyfriend," because submitting to a boyfriend is a lower level of commitment. Your commitment to Jesus should be without reservation, as it should be to a husband. The key to living successfully as a single Christian woman is to understand that you're serving your holy Husband. This is the path of holiness within singleness for a woman, and happiness is a by-product of holiness. (See Nancy Kaser's book *CROWN* for a great explanation of this.)

Fully embracing your role as His bride will remove much of the perceived loneliness during this time. Not only have you been set aside for His special, holy purposes (Heb. 10:10), but He is also telling you that during this time He simply wants you all to Himself. Sisters, isn't that what we want, a man who will move mountains to have us all to himself? During this time of singleness, your priority is serving your Man—the Son of Man, the title He calls Himself more than any other. Assuming your heart is His during this time, He is delighting in your full attention. And with that, He may also be preparing you for your next big mission trip for Him. That's why it's important to have the right view of those potential next stages.

Marriage is like a mission trip. Nobody boards a plane to fly around the world on a mission without some preparation. Jumping into a marriage without proper preparation during your season of singleness is like jumping on a plane to fly to a third-world country with no clothes, money, accompaniment, overnight arrangements, transportation, or specified purpose for service. Although initially it sounds fun, adventurous, and spontaneous (maybe even romantic), you'll soon become vulnerable, hungry, disillusioned, and of little service to anyone. The purpose for marriage is to glorify God through the relationship, and you may be in a season of preparation for this calling. The best way to do this? Glorify God in the relationship you have with Him during singleness. Learning what this looks like now gives you the critical compass you'll need should you step into the marriage mission field later.

Practically speaking, what does single submission look like? Let's look at the single women in Jesus's life and see what they did. While Jesus wasn't married, there were women who followed Him and the disciples and dedicated their lives to serving Him. They did so in heart and soul dedication, but it's also clear that they did so quietly—until His resurrection. There isn't a lot of Scripture written about these women, but consider the brief passage in Luke 8:1–3 acknowledging their service:

> After this, Jesus traveled about from one town and village to another, proclaiming the good news of the kingdom of God. The Twelve were with him, and also some women who had been cured of evil spirits and diseases: Mary (called Magdalene) from whom seven demons had come out; Joanna the wife of Chuza, the manager of Herod's household; Susanna; and many others. These women were helping to support them out of their own means.

I believe these women were critical to the success of the most important mission ever, and they were used simply because they were willing to follow and serve Him in dedication, even though none of them was His wife. Their hearts of gratitude drove them into this service because of what He had done for them. This beautiful and often undiscussed service of the women on that mission happened entirely because of the willing submission of these mostly single women. Interestingly, according to the passage, Joanna was married, but she was at least temporarily parted from her husband, Chuza, during this time and was able to travel with and serve Jesus.

So this powerful and understated group of mostly single women followed Jesus and the disciples, traveling with, tending to, and supporting Jesus's ministry in the ways they could. They simply did what they could do to serve because they recognized that Jesus was worth devoting their lives to.

And, my sisters, what was their reward for this quiet time of service? They became the first to witness the proof of the greatest miracle that has ever occurred—the resurrection of Jesus Christ. They became the first to speak of it to the world (Mark 16:1; John 20:1; Luke 24:1–11). Do you realize that the women who served Jesus and did so quietly without the need for a spotlight, fame, or recognition were the very ones used to first proclaim the resurrection? I have great confidence that these women were not out bragging about all the works they did while they served Jesus or trying to sell His autograph. I know for sure they weren't taking sexy selfies by the Sea of Galilee to remind everyone on social media that they were single and "in service." They just followed Him for the reward of being close to Him and showing their gratitude. In turn, they became the first evangelists to declare the newly open access to heaven available through Jesus. No earthly husband can compare to that reward. A little perspective goes a long way for us all.

So, single sister, go serve, and do so quietly with a gentle and humble spirit (1 Peter 3:4). Your Father in heaven knows all your needs (Matt. 6:8). Do your work in this season as though for the Lord. Cook your dinner and wash those dishes as though you had prepared them with Him by your side, because He is. Light a candle and eat with Him by that candlelight. He's not going to complain about anything you cook, even if you only have cereal for dinner. Drive yourself to church and sing all the way there because He's next to you enjoying that joyful noise no matter what joy, or lack thereof, it brings to anyone else. Go home and talk to Him about your day. Journal, listen, and take time to purposely make room in your life for His response. Believe me, this is a great season to do so. Ask Him about the movies you should watch, books you should read, entertainment you should seek, and friends you should be around.

241

Ask Him where you're most needed to serve others. Ask Him to bring you whom He wants you to spend time with in this season.

What you hear in instruction, obey. What you receive in blessing, give back to Him. This is the simplistic beauty of submission. Don't get in the way of all He has for you by thinking your strategy will get you to your next place sooner. The key to being single is to act like you're not—at least not by worldly standards. Single sister, this is not a place of independence as the world would tell you. If you're a Christian, you have someone to answer to besides yourself. If you've accepted Jesus as your Savior, you have no reason to act like you're single. You've got the only perfect Husband in the world, and He's waiting in delightful anticipation to see how you're going to serve Him in this season.

Submission in Togetherness— as a Girlfriend

I've got great news for you. If you're now someone's girlfriend or fiancée and you've done the single stage as described in service and submission to your holy Husband, you're already halfway through the lessons of the girlfriend stage and in great preparation for the oneness stage of marriage. Your foundation was set properly, and now you just need to implement those same practices with another person involved in your relationship with Jesus. Note that I said that another person becomes involved in your already-established relationship, the relationship between you and Jesus that *is already* rock solid. Don't leave that critical relationship to form a relationship with another person and leave Jesus as the outlier. The purpose of doing it this way is so Jesus Himself can be the one to kick that boyfriend out the door if he's not the right one. At this stage, you invite this new man into your already-established "house" with Jesus. You don't build a new one yet.

One of the most important moments of this for me was in the first stages of my relationship with my husband. As referenced earlier, we met online and enjoyed conversation with one another, but were both initially concerned about the three-hour distance between us. Neither wanted a long-distance relationship, and since we were both raising kids in established schools, neither had the desire to relocate. There was no foreseeable solution, but we couldn't deny that we wanted to explore the relationship further.

Geoff asked me one night on the phone, "So we are obviously geographically challenged here. What do you want to do about it?"

My response surprised even me (thank you, Holy Spirit!). I replied, "Well, you're the man. I'll let you take the lead."

Geoff recalls that at that moment his heartstrings were strummed in a way he had experienced with no other woman. I had left it up to Geoff to follow God appropriately and reflect that back to me in his leadership. It was up to God to direct the relationship properly in response to Geoff's willing submission to Him.

I have frequently heard one of my pastors, Ryan Vanderwarker, remind the flock, "If Jesus has handled our most important need, the need for salvation, then we can trust Him to handle the other details of life." I knew He could handle my dating relationship, but the act of my submission in itself revealed to Geoff that it was worthwhile proceeding to the next step in the relationship. Because this aligned with God's plan, my obedience in submission moved me right out of the 175-mile friend zone and eventually into my husband's house in Virginia. Hallelujah!

Remember, though, submission is always an issue of the heart. You can't fake submission just by saying things to indicate headship in a relationship. Submission used in any other form, especially as the means to manipulate, is not submission to Jesus but submission to Satan. Your heart has to fully embrace Jesus before submission can reveal His plan for you and His blessings in your obedience.

This, my sister, is the key to submission as a girlfriend. Start giving the man you're with the taste of headship and unconditional respect that he desires as a man of God. Allow him to provide direction for the relationship and its pace. Allow him to begin to consider on his own what his role and responsibility will be should he want to proceed further into the role of your husband. You do not need to spell all this out for him. A man of God should be just that—a man, not a boy. If you find yourself treating him like a boy, either you haven't embraced biblical submission or you aren't dating a man.

A man of God allows God to promote him as your husband and first seeks *His* permission. The world may tell you he should have your earthly daddy's permission (and that may be a nice idea), but no permission is more critical than your heavenly Father's, your original Husband. Jesus's allowing this man to take on the role of earthly husband to you isn't just for your provision. It's a necessary part of your sanctification, and only He knows what you need for that journey.

Your job at this important stage is to fully submit in the appropriate ways to this man in your life, respecting him as a brother in Christ and as a potential husband, and to stand securely as the guard over your heart and your boundaries as a still-single Christian woman. You aren't married, which means this man doesn't get access to your bank account or your possessions—and certainly not your precious body—before taking the vow. He doesn't get to make huge life decisions for you if he hasn't made a lifetime commitment to you and the Lord first. While you may show him great respect and convey admiration for him by asking his opinion on various choices you may need to make during this time, be careful to understand that you aren't required to submit to his direction yet. More importantly, you definitely shouldn't submit if he directs you in any sort of sinful manner. Don't blur the lines just because he makes plans to make a commitment. "Putting a ring on it" doesn't secure access; it just makes a reservation for it. Don't be fooled. The ring doesn't mean anything without the vow.

This is a crucial time to show him that you intend to do things God's way and you expect that he will want the same and will support you in that. This is also the time that reveals if he really is able and willing to commit to that. If this isn't the man God intends to be your husband, God may still use you as a critical sister in his life to prepare him for that stage in the future with someone else. But if this is the man God intends for you to marry, so much understanding of your life together will come to you at this time. Don't underestimate how much you will learn about your future husband in this critical stage of "togetherness" prior to marriage.

While most of this book is directed toward sisters during a period of singleness, I want to share what submission looks like in the next phase of oneness as a wife, because it's important to understand the distinctions. Remember, even if earthly marriage isn't in God's specific plan for you, we are all called to lifetime ministry—one way or another—as brides of Christ.

SUBMISSION IN ONENESS—AS A WIFE

"Togetherness" (dating) isn't the time to build a new house. "Oneness" is that time. Marriage is the time to create a brand-new "house" that is home to the new relationship, an unbreakable cord of three that entwines you, your husband, and God (Eccl. 4:12) at the time of your vows.

This house should be a sanctuary, and as a wife you have great charge and influence over the elements impacting that home on the inside and outside (Prov. 31:10-31). While you're not the head of your house, you're the one with a unique and important perspective on how that house is built, maintained, and secured. As second in charge, don't underestimate your influence on the stability of your new house.

I'm learning so much, most of it by the mistakes I make as a wife. Day by day it's a progressive dying to self to serve my God by serving my human husband. My job in submission actually becomes more important in the tougher times. Marriage is a tougher time, by the way (1 Cor. 7:28). Our faith is similarly tested when we have to be one with another person instead of being focused on ourselves. This is why it's so important to aim to be one with God prior to this stage so you truly know what that should look like and can mirror it well in the midst of everything else you'll be doing.

Aside from the blessing of God-blessed sex in this stage, there will be other things you'll be doing in your new role of biblically submissive wife. The term for that role is *helpmate* or *helper*, and as many commentaries point out, the word *helper* is the same one used by Jesus to refer to the role of the Holy Spirit (John 14:26).

Nothing can create a more ineffective and distasteful helper than one whose bitter heart is trying to fake submission, hide resentment, or cover up her disappointment over her husband's perceived failures. And that is most often revealed through our fiery tongue. For me, biblical submission for a wife is most clearly demonstrated by control of the tongue.

Sisters, there's no pulpit here. I'm talking to myself as well. Oh, my wicked, wicked tongue disguised by the pretty red lipstick that never fails to surround it. This wicked weapon has come out to cut my husband more times than I'd ever wish to remember. I could do well keeping my body in shape, my skin nice, my makeup fresh, perfume lingering, and hair done, but when that wicked mouth spews its poison, the rest is undone by one of the smallest members of the body (James 3:5) quicker than I can lose a press-on nail tip. And the consequence always comes with much more damage than I'm prepared to handle.

There's such value in embracing what the book of James says about the tongue, especially as it relates to biblical submission in marriage:

> We all stumble in many ways. Anyone who is never at fault in what they say is perfect, able to keep their whole body in check. Likewise, the tongue is a small part of the body, but it makes great boasts. Consider what a great forest is set on fire by a small spark. The tongue also is a fire, a world of evil among the parts of the body. It corrupts the whole body, sets the whole course of one's life on fire, and is itself set on fire by hell.
> (James 3:2, 5–6)

James is explaining that the tongue reveals the condition of the whole body. It can set a person's entire life ablaze, and is fueled by hell itself. I need to take that as seriously as it's intended. If I'm not careful, I can allow my passion to ruin all the good things it could accomplish. It can hurt me and burn up my whole life and everyone close to me. Submitting our tongue to God is one of the most important things we can do to serve our husbands (and our Lord) during this time.

Why does it sound like I'm implying that mastery of the tongue is more critical in this stage than during singleness and togetherness? It's because you've taken a God-confirmed vow in holy matrimony to serve your earthly husband and to be a helpmate mirroring the holy standard of the ultimate helper, the Holy Spirit. You've become one flesh with another person, which means you can no longer prevent your words and actions from impacting him. You may be more tempted to "let it fly" as you've experienced months, and maybe years, of unexpected hardships, disappointments, or misunderstandings common in marriage, but this is when your previous preparation of living holy despite your feelings will be critical. This is when your service as a holy helpmate is most needed. And this is the time when you can do the most damage, burning you both with the flames of your tongue. There should be nothing that taints that important role you've adopted as his helpmate, and you simply can't handle the risk that a fiery tongue creates in a marriage—like a toddler playing alone with matches in the living room.

The Bible says that a foolish woman will tear down her house with her own hands (Prov. 14:1). This foolishness reveals a wicked heart, and our tongues are often the most prominent and most dangerous manifestation of a wicked heart. That tongue in your mouth is rooted in the heart, and out of the overflow of your heart, it will speak (Luke 6:45). Set your heart right before God by being in submission first to Him and then to your husband so that when the tongue reveals the overflow, it is lovely, biblically submitted, and reflective of a good God, who has given your husband the good gift of you.

THE ULTIMATE BENEFITS OF SUBMISSION

While we've moved through a taste of what biblical submission looks like in these various stages, I want to leave you with the understanding of the incredible benefits of submission. There are two huge—but rarely mentioned—benefits of submission that should be powerful motivators.

First, you're not responsible for the results that come from being submissive. Given the heavy weight of responsibility that women carry in modern society, can we all embrace this reality for a moment? If you do what God commands with a genuinely submissive, joyful, and grateful heart regardless of your circumstance, then you're not responsible for the outcome.

So if you're single and do exactly what God commands you to do and you lose your job, you can be sure He's got it covered. It's part of His plan for your life. If you're in a relationship and do exactly what you're supposed to but the relationship ends, you can be sure that God has moved him out of the way to make room for a better one. If you're a married woman and do all you should do and submit to your husband's authority in your home, but his direction leads you into difficulty, you can be sure that God will hold him accountable for what he's done with you both.

Without sounding like I'm excited about it not being my job to ensure the result, I can tell you I'm excited about it not being my job! My job is already outlined, almost like an employee of a company. When I do my job well, I'm not responsible if the company succeeds or not. I don't have that pressure on me. Thanks be to God. Listen, sisters, I'm simply rejoicing in the fact that Jesus lined it up so that we wouldn't have more pressure on us. He knew exactly what the trajectory of our lives would be, and He knew the challenges both brothers and sisters in Christ would face during this tumultuous time.

God was gracious enough to give us the Ten Commandments so we would clearly know our boundaries, but Jesus summed them up in two so we don't need to feel overwhelmed. He simply said to love Him and love others like we want to be loved (Matt. 22:37–40). Sisters, to stay in submission and reap the benefits, we simply need to stay in Christ under His protective, encompassing umbrella of love.

As if the ultimate disclaimer of responsibility for the results weren't enough of a benefit to motivate the biblical submission of a believer, there's one other aspect that no one could debate as the ultimate benefit.

Biblical submission aligns you most closely to the character and person of your Lord and Savior, Jesus Christ. I'd argue that there is no other physical, mental, or emotional aspect of Jesus that we can align with more than an attitude of holy submission. As women, we can't claim to look like Jesus did as a man, even though we are made in God's image (Gen. 1:27). We can't claim to think like He did because our thoughts aren't His (Isa. 55:8). But we can relate directly in the area of temptation because the Bible states that He was tempted in all the ways we are (Heb. 4:15), yet chose to submit to His Father. He has given us all ability to follow His example (2 Peter 1:3) and proceed in obedience.

Jesus chose submission as a means of maintaining unity with His Father so that we could understand He was modeling the same relationship potential for us. Remember, He promises that as we obey and submit, we will come closer to Him and He in turn will draw nearer to us (James 4:8). Submission in its purest form reflects unity with God, as it mirrors holiness. Submission is as close to heaven as we can get on earth. There can be no greater benefit than this.

Sister, if you're still not convinced, let's get back to one of our favorite subjects. I can tell you that there's nothing better in your physical body than the experience of biblically submissive sex with the husband God has chosen for you specifically. Just to be clear, I'm not talking about ungodly forms of submission. (For example, there's nothing biblical about the unholy submission described in books such as *Fifty Shades of Grey*. Again, check out Shannon Ethridge's book *The Fantasy Fallacy* for a great perspective on disarming this phenomenon.) But I can tell you from personal experience that holy sex in submission to Jesus—the One who has formed every part of your body and knows every nerve, every curve, and every desire—has the ability to deliver much more than our minds or hearts can even fathom in this life (Eph. 3:20).

This is the most amazing sexual experience you can have on this earth, and it doesn't depend on your husband's abilities or interests. Does that mean that sex with your husband will always be a knockdown, mind-blowing experience simply because he also loves God? Not likely. Does that mean that your husband will physically transform into the image of Christ as you make love? Not likely. But when Jesus is present and you experience His presence because of your willingness to submit in love to your role, there's nothing like the physical sensation of Him. I had heard this was the case. I was determined to find out for sure. Read on to the next chapter. The life of a biblically submissive wife is full of blessings beyond our imagining, and biblically submissive sex is just one awesome aspect of that!

CHAPTER 10

Determining the Worth: Written from the Other Side

If I had cherished sin in my heart,
    the Lord would not have listened;
but God has surely listened
    and has heard my prayer.
Praise be to God,
    who has not rejected my prayer
    or withheld his love from me!
(Ps. 66:18–20)

It's April 1, 2017. God has brought me through the valley, and from the mountaintop I see that there was light in that valley after all. I didn't always see it, but my body feels it now. I'm stronger.

I'm confident in Christ. I'm wearing a white wedding gown and meaning every thread of it for the first time in my life because of my redemption. Today I'll become a Christian wife. I've never felt more precious in God's sight. I'm not the person I was five years ago.

On this day I will walk down the aisle arm in arm with Jesus to the man with whom I will become one flesh. This moment is as pure and joyful as can be because of the endurance and bond created through our temporary suffering together for His sake. It's in this moment that I realize how very worthwhile it was. The moment is unblemished. It's like the feeling between finishing in first place in a marathon and receiving the trophy. As you bask in the light of victory, just knowing you've achieved it takes away some of the desperation you might have previously felt. You know you will soon receive the trophy, but in the meantime the satisfaction is already largely realized. Don't get me wrong; I knew the prize would be magnificent, but I was unprepared for the fulfillment I would receive having finished well with my Savior by my side. I am radiant with peace and joy and confidence as I receive my husband, Geoff.

The memory of what happened on my wedding night is not something I can fully describe or share with anyone. It was the most sacred, palpable, Holy Spirit moment of my life, and I don't dare discredit any portion of it with my human words.

Sisters, I didn't exaggerate for a dramatic ending. I honestly believe it was the very closest to heaven that I'll reach on this earth. The pleasure of orgasm doesn't even compare to the pleasure of the Holy Spirit in the midst of my husband and me for the first time. There truly are no words to describe it. I have never ever felt more beautiful, loved, divinely attended to, and blessed in purity than I did at that moment. If just one reader is inspired by my honest testimony here, it will have been worth every moment invested in sharing my story and getting through the dark nights to tell it.

Despite the struggles of the past, I was in awe to realize that this moment of victory with my husband wasn't about our sexual compatibility or chemistry or the release of pent-up sexual energy. In fact, what occurred was something distinctly different and far better from sexuality (and that's a big deal coming from someone who loves sex). Remember how I said that during celibacy other senses heighten in different ways? Well, when my husband and I came together and experienced God-blessed sex for the first time, every one of my senses heightened in ways that I didn't expect. The level of euphoria was absolutely at the point of verging on too much. In this moment, every single second of pain, stress, frustration, longing, impatience, questioning, and struggle became fully justified and worthwhile. Every single second of it. Knowing in my heart that the experience of heaven is better—in direct communion with my Savior—my mind simply can't fathom that level of ecstasy. I honestly can't fathom more than what I experienced then on my wedding night.

If you've read nothing else in this book but skipped ahead to this section to see if reading the rest of the book and following its advice was worthwhile, please hear this. As I said at the beginning, I don't expect this to reach the whole world. I only want it to go to whomever God intended to hear this. Even if that's just one person. Just for you? It is worth it!

I never planned on writing this book because I never planned on being the kind of person who would write a "crazy" book about the value of submitting to God or seeking sexual purity. These notions were absolutely ludicrous in my mind. The fact that you're holding this book, that I typed these words, that I chose to endure celibacy and pursue sexual purity all the way up the aisle to my husband—none of these were my doing or would have been my choice if the Holy Spirit hadn't changed and empowered me from the inside out. I didn't want these changes. I just decided that I wanted Him, and all this changed with it.

I'm a living testimony of all I never thought I would live to be. To God alone be the glory.

Now does that mean that every Christian marriage, especially that of a husband and wife who have chosen to keep themselves "pure" prior to marriage, will have the most glorious sexual experience on their wedding night? I imagine it isn't so in every case. Our humanity and sin nature can mess up even the best things. Ever crash a brand-new car that was perfect until the moment you got in it?

But I do know that sex is God's gift to husband and wife as He unites them physically as one flesh. I know that I never experienced the notion of that one flesh in a godly way before my wedding night with Geoff, and I can tell you it was entirely different from any other sexual experience I've had. The one flesh that forms when God Himself smiles over you as He applies the ultimate bonding between husband and wife was an experience where, for me, He was more palpable, perhaps because my husband and I were more vulnerable. We were as ready for Him as we were for each other. When I'm ready to take my last breath, it's the memory of this moment with my husband that I pray leads me into eternity. I honestly wish this beautiful moment for every Christian married couple.

While I would like every married couple to experience this, the entire purpose of this book is to let you know that it's just not possible to experience Christ in this way without accepting Christ first. While Jesus is waiting for you to receive Him as Savior and bless your marriage, you will block His blessing by not welcoming

Him into it. And you can't welcome Him on your own terms. Our holy God doesn't need to submit. You do. That means there is no way of getting around it. If you want to experience God-blessed sex, then you have to get there God's way. It is a gift from Him alone, not something you can obtain on your own.

Sisters, there is something magnificent that happens in a woman's heart when she sees a man so dedicated to his Lord and to his bride that he is willing to make this temporary commitment to celibacy in order to lead appropriately to the altar. The Lord wants for you to walk up that aisle in all of His pure white glory, presented as a perfect gift to your new marriage and to your new husband. This is actually your husband's call in marriage as reflected in Ephesians 5:25–28:

> Husbands, love your wives, just as Christ loved the church and gave himself up for her to make her holy, cleansing her by the washing with water through the word, and to present her to himself as a radiant church, without stain or wrinkle or any other blemish, but holy and blameless. In this same way, husbands ought to love their wives as their own bodies.

If he's not committed to doing this before marriage, don't expect that he'll be committed after you're married.

This may sound harsh, but it's not something you can be in denial about. Don't confuse your love for him, or his for you, as a reason to justify graying areas that are black and white. That doesn't mean that you or your man will be perfect in all your actions, but it does mean that you pursue God with an undivided heart. His way is clear, without stain, wrinkle, or other blemish.

REDEMPTION IS STILL POSSIBLE

So what happens if you've already fallen to sexual temptation with your spouse before marriage or with someone else before meeting your spouse? Well, I've taken both paths and can tell you from experience that we have an awesome God who redeems us when we're ready to submit. If you're alive, breathing, and reading this, it's not too late.

I was sexually active prior to meeting my first husband, and he and I didn't choose God's path for our dating or marriage relationship. In fact, I didn't actively seek God at any time during my first marriage—unless I was in trouble. Then I was begging for Him to help me. It was never a sincere desire for relationship, only for blessing. Had my first husband and I sincerely repented and submitted to the Lord as a couple, our marriage might not have ended.

But when I found the Lord after my first marriage, I sincerely wanted Him in every way, even while enduring intense temptation. He provided me the undeserved blessing of a second chance to experience things His way. We're never guaranteed a second chance, no matter how right our hearts get. But there's always, always, hope in Christ.

If you and your spouse fell into temptation before getting married, there may be some emotional scars that need healing, but God can redeem anything. The Bible tells us to repent, confess, and seek Him together in unity as husband and wife. The Lord will bless sincere hearts that seek Him. Seek to be healed entirely from the sexual sin; confess to the Lord, confess to each other, and ask God to purify your relationship to fully glorify Him. Read the Word together, pray together, and seek in all ways to please the Lord. Persevere. Seek to be of one mind in unity with Him, and God will bless your one flesh. Remember, the Bible says that when we seek first the kingdom and His righteousness, all else will be provided for us (Matt. 6:33).

Remember how I originally started out seeking the best sex possible? I found it and can say with absolute certainty that the best sex possible is God-blessed sex. There is no comparison. The delight and satisfaction is deeper than any other fleshly experience and lasts well beyond when the physical encounter is done. I'm writing this to celebrate with you. Whether you're there now or potentially on your way, know that the celebration is abundantly more than you can ask or think (Eph. 3:20). Even then, it's just a small taste of heaven.

THE TRUTH ABOUT WORTH

I'm sure you wanted to know whether celibacy was worth it. The answer, from my human perspective, is a resounding yes. But I'm unqualified to write this from the more important eternal perspective because there's something I just don't know, and it's found in Romans 8:18 (NLT):

> Yet what we suffer now is nothing compared to the glory He will reveal to us later.

Even though I found amazing blessings through this particular trial and indeed confirm that it was a worthwhile pursuit, I still do consider it to have been a great challenge. I can't grasp how the trials I've faced or the other more serious trials that others have faced could become "nothing" as this Scripture declares. My mind can't process something so great as to wipe the slate of hardship entirely clean just by comparison. So if you've picked up this book looking for the answer, you've just got it. There's nothing we can go through—and suffer for Christ—that will have permanent hardship attached to it in this temporary life. So even if you spend the rest of your life celibate in dedication to the Lord, what you face will be "nothing" compared to what's coming. In our suffering, believers are being prepared for that which will render it all more than worthwhile.

While I appreciate the opportunity to share my experience, it's more important that you hear from Him about the worth of sexual purity. According to Romans 8:18, my limited human perspective doesn't give justice to fully answering the question of worth because I can't count, fathom, or imagine—from an eternal perspective—the full value of obedience to God. I wrote this book to others, but my testimony can't compare to the truth and eternal reassurance in the Word. If you've spent time reading this book and haven't spent time reading the Bible recently, I honestly ask that you do that now.

Committing to God's path of obedience for sexual purity was one of the greatest trials of my whole life, and it was one I only got through because I pursued Jesus more than anything else. Harnessing my passion for Jesus rather than for myself led me to the secondary blessing of sexual bliss. It also allowed me to realize the fruit of the Spirit in a way I never had before, especially that of self-control.

This fast from sexual impurity taught me more about how He's made me than I ever realized before as well. It opened my eyes to catch a glimpse of what is really possible when He's at the center of a life and, even better, when He's at the center of a relationship. The benefits have extended so far beyond a sexual realm. I don't fear things the way I used to because when I know I can't do something due to my fear, inability, insecurity, or lack of desire, I know He can and will empower me to do so if He commands it. Making it through the temptation together was an incredible bonding experience that allowed me to see just how much I could depend on and trust the God-fearing man whom I was marrying. It also taught me a lot about myself. Walking the path to pursue sexual purity redefined a new level of Philippians 4:13 for me personally: "I can do all this through Him who gives me strength."

I'm able to choose joy more freely because I've learned that it's a choice. Without so much emphasis on living a self-centered life, I've truly experienced the freedom in Christ that so many people talk about. While I don't walk perfectly in the Spirit each day, I'm free from the chains that bound me. Those chains were lies that convinced me that I was enslaved by my passionate desires and would be unfulfilled without quenching them first. I'm free of the burden to live my life according to the desires of the flesh because God has given me the desires of my heart.

And nothing can ever take the victory from me because it was always the victory of Christ alone. I in Him, and Him in me (John 15:4). And there is never a sweeter, more worthwhile place to be this side of heaven.

CHAPTER 11

Fireplace: The Lovely Way to Burn

For this reason I remind you to fan into flame the gift of God, which is in you through the laying on of my hands.
(2 Tim. 1:6)

My parents named me after a song about a woman who consumed her lover in such a way that even long after she had left him he continued to find glory in the short, but intense, way she had loved him. It was like my parents knew I would love with a fierceness that could not be contained, that would subject me—and those around me—to a thousand deaths by my own hand. They knew before I was born. This has been a long journey.

I spent many years trying to figure out my intense passion, wrestling with it, even trying to extinguish it by choking out its oxygen. I didn't realize there was indeed a healthy place for it. In fact, I felt like each time I looked around this world, I could only see that there was no place for it where it wouldn't set flame to those around it as well.

If you've decided to read this far, there's probably something ringing true inside you in terms of your own passion. I know I'm not talking to everyone, but rather to those women out there who, like me, just don't know what to do with all the emotions that stir inside. You're not alone, and you were not created for anything outside His purpose. All things, most especially you, were made by Him and for His glory (personal application added from Col. 1:16). The desire of my heart is that you have read enough to know that not all flame is bad.

Only three letters differentiate the words *rest* and *wrestle*. While their meanings are almost opposite, we often confuse the purpose of the two. As Christians, we claim to know that we are to rest in Christ, but the reality is that we spend more time wrestling. What's interesting to me is that the word *rest* is situated right inside the word that means practically its opposite. Can we rest in the midst of the struggle? Thus far in my life, I've spent more time wrestling with the fire than resting with it or in it. The time has come for a shift.

I hadn't viewed my intense passion as much of a gift before, especially since it got me in more and more trouble as I followed it. But now I see it as a gift. My passion is what has driven me to finish this book and, God willing, hopefully inspire you with my testimony. My passion is what gives me endurance and drive to persevere, to finish well in all areas of my walk, and to meet Him at the finish line.

The problem was never my passion. It was that I was following it instead of directing it to the place where it was safe and even desirable. It needed to be contained to an area—like a fireplace—where it could produce all the beauty, warmth, and purpose it was created for rather than taking down the whole house with it. It didn't need an extinguisher; it needed a divine director.

When I found the verse at the beginning of this chapter, 2 Timothy 1:6, I was especially moved. Paul is giving Timothy, his beloved son in the faith, clear direction for ministry. Paul is instructing Timothy to "fan into flame" the gift of God in him. Although Paul also wrote 1 Corinthians 7:9 warning against the burn (being consumed by fiery lust), here in 2 Timothy, Paul is using the analogy of fire in a positive sense to inspire Timothy to a passionate obedience in his mission for Christ. Paul's exhortation shows that the flame just needs to be used in the appropriate way.

On a more personal note, my name, Joanna, actually means "gift of God." So just looking at the first part of this verse, I once again hear my God whispering part of His plan to me. As my ultimate Father, He would fan me into flame with passion and plans for me before I was born (Jer. 1:5). He was just waiting for me to look to Him to learn how to burn in a way that was lovely—in a way that would bless and not harm His kingdom. Looking back, I absolutely believe I was always meant to be on fire. I absolutely believe He approved of the name given to me by His grace. I smile and relate when I read the verse, "But by the grace of God I am what I am, and His grace to me was not without effect," as Paul writes in 1 Corinthians 15:10.

I encourage you to personalize the Word of God in your own life, walk, and purpose if you haven't already done so. Scripture is meant to show you all truth. Take His Word, ask Him to show you what it means for your walk with Him in this life, personally, and then embrace and fan into flame all that He's gifted you with, to proceed with His divine direction. The Bible may be the most widely published book in history, but it's the most personal thing ever written. Your personal love letter from the Creator of the entire universe awaits, hidden for you within its pages. I did not know this was true until I read it for myself.

While I have by no means met any standard of perfection in submission or in using my passion in only perfectly appropriate ways, I have stopped wrestling with its place in my life. It's only by the grace and peace of God that I can safely put down the fire extinguisher now, knowing that what's burning isn't a surprise or a danger to myself or those around me.

God is burning off all the dross in me by my willingness to submit my passion for His purpose. Having truly submitted to Him, the only place my fire is now dangerous is to the enemy of my soul, because he can't use it against me anymore. It's him now trying desperately to get hold of that extinguisher instead of me, but it's a losing battle because he can't extinguish what's already rooted in eternity.

So, fire woman, have you been rooted? Have you been contained? Have you been divinely directed to the place where He wants you to burn with more passion for Him than all the others around you? Have you been placed where you can be used to be a steadfast burning light? Or are you trying to suppress what really should just be fanned into flame in the appropriate way?

Put down the extinguisher. Grab His hand, grab the Word, and go boldly, brightly, hotly, and intensely to the very place where He is directing and using your passion for Him and not against you. He is for you. His gifts are so good. Fan them. Into flame.

Fire Women Resources

Dannah Gresh, *And the Bride Wore White: Seven Secrets to Sexual Purity*

Greg Speck, *Sex: It's Worth Waiting For*

Jonathan McKee, *Sex Matters*

Jonathan McKee, *The Guy's Guide to God, Girls, and the Phone in Your Pocket*

Francis and Lisa Chan, *You and Me Forever: Marriage in Light of Eternity*

Nancy Kaser, *CROWN: 30 Wife-Changing Lessons*

Shannon Ethridge, *The Fantasy Fallacy: Exposing the Deeper Meaning behind Sexual Thoughts*

The Biblical Counseling Foundation, *bcfministries.org*

The Holy Bible

Tim Alan Gardner, *Sacred Sex: A Spiritual Celebration of Oneness in Marriage*

Share Your Experience

FireWomenBook.com

@ FireWomenBook

About the Author

Joanna Sanders is a graduate of Villanova University and Moody Theological Seminary. She's the founder and head writer of Colossians46.com, which provides biblical content support, writing, and editing. She loves helping other authors realize God's purpose through their stories and reflecting His glory back through their words. It has been her lifelong dream to finally write her own story. Joanna writes and edits for several Christian publications and publishers and has a heart for women's ministry.

Most importantly, she is wife to Geoff and mom to three godly-men-in-training. Cookies, pasta, music, and the beach also play integral roles in her life.

Order Information

To order additional copies of this book,
please visit www.firewomenbook.com.
Also available on Amazon.com and
BarnesandNoble.com.

Made in the USA
Lexington, KY
22 November 2019